University of Kansas Publications
Humanistic Studies, No. 35

SIX STUDIES IN NINETEENTH-CENTURY ENGLISH LITERATURE AND THOUGHT

SIX STUDIES IN NINETEENTH-CENTURY ENGLISH LITERATURE AND THOUGHT

edited by

Harold Orel and George J. Worth

Contributors:

W. P. ALBRECHT
HAROLD OREL
WALTER E. SANDELIUS
GEORGE J. WORTH
PETER CAWS
W. D. PADEN

UNIVERSITY OF KANSAS PUBLICATIONS
LAWRENCE, 1962

PREFACE

This collection of essays by various members of the faculty of the University of Kansas is, we hope, of interest to students of the nineteenth century.

There is something new, and perhaps something important, in each of these discussions. We hope, above all, that they convey a sense of the abundant excitement which we find in this period.

H. O.
G. W.

Contents

Hazlitt on Wordsworth; or, The Poetry of Paradox

by W. P. Albrecht

The "poetry of paradox," says Hazlitt, "had its origin in the French revolution, or rather in those sentiments and opinions which produced that revolution. . . ." It was founded "on a principle of sheer humanity, on pure nature void of art." Although always a great defender of the French Revolution, humanity, and nature, especially as the gauge of art, Hazlitt put the poetry of paradox at the bottom of a scale of excellence down which English poetry had been sliding since the Renaissance. From "the poetry of imagination, in the time of Elizabeth," he says, poetry declined "by successive gradations" to "the poetry of paradox" in his own time.[1]

Much of contemporary poetry seemed "paradoxical" to Hazlitt, but most often his "poets of paradox" are the Lake School, especially Wordsworth. "The paradox [these poets] set out with was, that all things are by nature equally fit subjects for poetry; or that if there is any preference to be given, those that are the meanest and most unpromising are the best, as they leave the greatest scope for the unbounded stores of thought and fancy in the writer's own mind." It is in this sense, not in any political one, that the paradoxical poets leveled distinctions and, in an excess of revolutionary zeal, flouted "authority and fashion."[2] Indeed, the fact that the chief practitioners of paradox had turned against the French Revolution, and against Hazlitt as well, may suggest that Hazlitt's evaluation of the poetry of paradox was not entirely disinterested. This was the view of Wordsworth, who in 1817 wrote to Haydon that "the miscreant Hazlitt continues . . . his abuse of Southey Coleridge and myself. . . ." A hundred years later Hazlitt's old enemy *Blackwood's Magazine* asserted the "whimsical paradox" that "Hazlitt, a Jacobin in politics, was a violent anti-Jacobin in literature."[3] This proposition is acceptable only if "anti-Jacobin" is adequately defined. The *Blackwood's* article proceeds to confuse Hazlitt's literary anti-Jacobinism with the abuse of "Wordsworth's private character," but the paradoxes in Hazlitt's position may be resolved without recourse to his personal or political disputes: Hazlitt is not guilty of his own charge against the "Ministerial Press" of making "literature the mere tool . . . of party-spirit,"[4] nor is he repudiating the French Revolution, humanity, or nature.

Hazlitt's dislike for Wordsworth's and Coleridge's politics is distinguishable from his evaluation of their poetry, just as his attacks on Scott the Tory are distinct from his admiration of Scott the novelist. Although he

1

singled out the paradoxical elements for disapproval, Hazlitt admired a great deal of Wordsworth's poetry; in fact, he placed Wordsworth "at the head of the poets of the present day, or rather . . . in a totally distinct class of excellence." Hazlitt, as Wellek has pointed out, recognized "the best of his time remarkably well"; and shortly after Hazlitt's death T. N. Talfourd could write in the *Examiner* that, despite his personal bitterness toward Wordsworth and Coleridge, only Hazlitt "has done justice to the immortal works of the one, and the genius of the other."[5] Thanks especially to Howe's *Life*, it is no longer as difficult as the Victorians found it to respect Hazlitt; but it is nevertheless pleasant to note how firm Hazlitt's critical principles stood against political pressures and personal abuse.

Hazlitt's literary anti-Jacobinism affirms, rather than rejects, his own political ideas. Probably better than any other part of his critical writings, Hazlitt's analysis of the poetry of paradox shows his belief that the good poet, like the good citizen, must fulfill the possibilities of his imagination: that poetic structure, like the best government, requires an escape from egotism into imaginative completeness. This principle is the key to Hazlitt's criticism of Wordsworth and other contemporaries. Occasionally, when Hazlitt expresses this principle in the commonplace terms of logic, decorum, and general nature, he may seem to apply it too harshly and mechanically; more often, however, the criterion of imaginative completeness leads Hazlitt to appreciate Wordsworth's excellence and to censure—in Wordsworth and others—what may justifiably be considered idiosyncrasy, bathos, and structural ineptitude. Hazlitt may sometimes, like many of his contemporaries, blur the distinctions between art and nature, but in his treatment of the poetry of paradox he takes a clear stand against subjectivism and formlessness, and insists that poetry attain a structured objectivity.

I

Hazlitt's general charge against the poets of his time is that they have gone to such extremes of subjectivity that they have failed to achieve either (1) a high degree of truth, (2) the means of poetic communication, or (3) both. Everywhere he finds a perverse individuality. Southey's "impressions are accidental, immediate, personal, instead of being permanent and universal." Shelley "trusted too implicitly to the light of his own mind. . . ." Keats, in *Endymion,* "painted his own thoughts and character. . . ." Byron is a "pampered egotist" who, instead of "bowing to the authority of nature, . . . only consults the . . . workings of his own breast, and gives them out as

2

oracles to the world." Landor's *Imaginary Conversations* is "a *chef-d'œuvre* of self-opinion and self-will. . . ." Landor and, to a lesser degree, Southey are the principal examples of that extreme form of paradox that Hazlitt calls "Literary Jacobinism." Hazlitt has a number of good things to say about the style, characterization, and humor in the *Imaginary Conversations,* but all is "defeated" by Landor's outrageous love of paradox that offends both reason and common sense.[6] At this point, Hazlitt's criticism of the poetry of paradox approaches a kind of commonplace logic-chopping, but his main concern is that the poets of paradox failed to consummate the imaginative process that great poetry exacts.

Hazlitt's principal criterion for literary excellence is *truth to nature,* and all the kinds of poetry inferior to the "poetry of imagination" fall short of "truth," in one way or another. Inferior poetry suffers, in other words, from "abstraction." The truth-finding faculty is imagination, and whatever limits its scope limits the poet's perception and representation of truth. The imagination is a combining faculty. In our perception of everyday phenomena, imagination immediately unites sensation with thought and feeling, and in poetry it continues to exert its amalgamating power in order to attain a still greater truth. Here its role is an objectifying and generalizing one. In a state of intense feeling the associations are more abundant; the imagination links the present with the past, summoning up thoughts and feelings which modify the present perception and give it the validity of repeated experience. Conditioned by past thoughts and feelings, the poet in a state of intense feeling immediately reaches "unpremeditated conclusions" of a high order of truth. Indispensable to the conditioning process is habitual sympathetic identification, which gives the poet's intuition of truth the validity of *common* experience. Emotion is important to the poet, therefore, both as a dimension of truth and as a condition in which he associates most copiously and, after proper conditioning by sympathetic identification, immediately arrives at "profound sentiments."[7]

The greatest poetry, Hazlitt believes, must not only comprise "profound sentiments" but also objectify these sentiments in generally moving images and exciting events. The state of feeling wherein the imagination defines the "internal character" or "the living principle" of its subject Hazlitt calls "gusto." This is also the state in which the imagination shapes the poet's experience into a work of art, selecting and combining those particulars that stimulate the reader's imagination to realize what is permanent and meaningful in human life.[8] Reviewing *The Excursion* in 1814, Hazlitt divides poetry

3

into "two classes; the poetry of imagination and the poetry of sentiment." The first arises "out of the faculties of memory and invention, conversant with the world of external nature; the other from the fund of our moral sensibility." Here Hazlitt uses the term "poetry of imagination" in a narrower sense than he usually does, for he apparently wants to emphasize the objectifying or externalizing power of imagination, its ability to fuse thoughts and feelings with concrete particulars. More frequently, as in describing Shakespeare's or Milton's poetry, he makes the "poetry of imagination" include high moral sensibility as well as excellent invention. In fact, in his review of *The Excursion,* he goes on to say that "the greatest poets . . . have been equally distinguished for richness of invention and depth of feeling." Since the days of Chaucer, Spenser, Shakespeare, and Milton the decline of poetry can be traced to the failure to combine "moral sensibility" and "fanciful invention." Young and Cowley possess the latter but not the former. ". . . Wordsworth, on the other hand, whose powers of feeling are of the highest order, is certainly deficient in fanciful invention: his writings exhibit all the internal power, without the external form of poetry."[9]

What keeps modern poets from fusing profound thoughts and feelings with striking images and events is their "bias to abstraction." The advance of civilization, which has made people less immediately responsive to the world of sensation, has blunted the powers of both feeling and invention; scientific progress has substituted inquiry and experiment for "immediate communication with nature"; and, more recently, the French Revolution has "distracted all hearts" from imaginative completion by centering people's attention on abstract principles of government and the "general nature of men and things. . . ."[10] For Hazlitt the best poetry demands self-fulfillment, for both the poet and the reader, in the sense that every area of possible emotional, intellectual, and moral response must remain open to the probings of association that are initiated by concrete particulars. This fulfillment is hindered "wherever an intense activity is given to any one faculty" at the expense of "the due and natural exercise of others." Intellectual activity in which "ideas of things" are divorced from pleasure or pain "must check the genial expansion of the moral sentiments and social affections, must lead to a cold and dry abstraction. . . ." When an object or idea is severed from its association with pain or pleasure, as it must be in scientific or syllogistic reasoning, it is devalued as material for poetry. For both poet and reader, the concrete particular, with its immediate emotional impact, must be allowed to initiate and enrich the flow of associations—especially those resulting from sympathetic identification—that modify perception and shape poetic truth. Other exclusive habits of mind, such as personal "vanity" or devotion to some philosophical or political scheme, have a similar effect on the imagination, excluding "profound sentiments" or preventing their expression in generally interesting images and events.[11] Since the poet must respond completely—in sensation, thought, and feeling—to the evocative experience, he must not interpose his will; he must not, like Shelley, discard "every thing as mystery and error for which he cannot account by an effort of mere intelligence," or, like Southey, lack the "patience to think that evil is inseparable from the nature of things," or, like Coleridge, "subject the Muse to *transcendental* theories. . . ."[12]

In Hazlitt, therefore, we find the same paradox as in Keats. Just as the denial of self that Keats calls negative capability must precede the affirmation of self that he calls soul-making, so must a high degree of sympathetic identification, and consequent loss of self, precede the self-fulfillment that Hazlitt defines as the poetic experience. Whether, as in Wordsworth, "egotism" makes every object in nature mirror the poet's own thoughts and feelings, or, as in Godwin, uses character and passion to "spin a subtle theory," or, as in Coleridge, "mistakes scholastic speculations for . . . passion," this egotism in poetry is "servile, inert, . . . stagnant. . . ." Keats and Hazlitt use similar metaphors to suggest the vitality and completeness of the imaginative experience when it is uninhibited by any abstracting or dividing egotism. Modern literature, says Hazlitt, "halts on one leg"; it does not—like Keats's bright-eyed, purposeful Stoat—"run on all fours." Modern poets, says Hazlitt, "are more in love with a theory than a mistress"; whereas in his "instinctiveness," says Keats, the poet should be like a Hawk or a Man "wanting a Mate. . . ." It is this absorption in a self-integrating or self-completing purpose that embodies poetic truth in striking particulars.[13] Neither Hazlitt nor, I think, Keats is insisting on the amorality of the imaginative process, not, at least, in any final sense. Douglas Bush has pointed out that what Keats opposes to "the wordsworthian or egotistical sublime" is "the impersonal, non-moral imagination of the poet of negative capability . . ."; but for Hazlitt, at least, the imaginative fusion includes morality: "impassioned poetry is an emanation of the moral and intellectual part of our nature, as well as of the sensitive—of the desire to know, the will to act, and the power to feel; and ought to appeal to these different parts of our constitution, in order to be perfect."[14] This emanation must, of course, come naturally through the process of excited but conditioned association. Apparently it must come as spontaneously and organically as the Ancient Mariner's blessing of the water-snakes, an act of unpremeditated but indisputable morality. The process of poetic creation, Hazlitt makes it clear, involves a moral response—conditioned by sympathetic identification—that leaves its mark on the final product, but he protests that any *premature* moralizing can only obstruct the process short of fruition.

As a political writer Hazlitt frequently objects to political ideas expressed in poems, plays, or novels; but when he considers a piece of writing as an imaginative work rather than a political document (and in Hazlitt's essays the distinction is not difficult to make), his objection is not to any particular set of ideas but to a writer allowing any ideas—political or otherwise—to control his imagination. His own political ideas, reduced to what Keats calls consequitive reasoning, are no more acceptable as material for poetry than anyone else's. "The cause of the people is indeed but ill calculated as a subject for poetry: it admits of rhetoric, which goes into argument and explanation, but it presents no immediate or distinct images to the mind. . . ." In fact, tyranny, if dramatized by striking and powerful characters like Coriolanus, will stimulate the imagination and prove more attractive and sympathetic than "abstract right." This does not mean, obviously, that literature must repudiate democratic ideas. "The spirit of poetry is in itself favourable to humanity and liberty. . . ."[15] In fact, both literature and the good society must be affirmations of individual freedom—achieved, not by reason alone, but by imaginative self-fulfillment. Like Hobbes and Locke, Hazlitt believes that each man is naturally free to pursue his selfish desires to the point where he would allow others the same freedom and that government exists to define this point and to restrain people from going beyond it. "Political justice" limits freedom according to the calculation of enlightened self-interest, but political justice may be achieved only in a context of "moral justice," which requires sympathetic identification with others achieved not by reason but by imagination, and sustained, as Rousseau believed, by the "virtue" as well as the "wisdom" of its citizens. A free society demands "the hand, heart, and head of the whole community acting to one purpose, with a mutual and thorough consent." Only under these conditions is the individual free in the sense that he makes the laws regulating his own behavior.[16]

Analogous, in its completeness, to the individual self-realization and communal integration of a democratic society is the experience provided by the greatest kind of poetry—tragedy—which offers a kind of freedom itself, as well as a means to realizing political freedom. Like "moral justice" tragedy integrates "the desire to know, the will to act, and the power to feel. . . ." The tragic poet does not, like Southey, overlook evil but represents it with all the truth of the imagination, so that the audience or reader enjoys not only intense *feeling* (hate as well as love) but also the power of *knowing* the thing he hates. Therefore, aware of the justness of the representation and of his feeling toward it, he is impelled to *act* accordingly. This self-realization (emotional, intellectual, moral) in the face of evil offers freedom, not from the consequences of evil—which are inescapable—but from being deceived by it. Political freedom is also advantaged. The audience may recognize and even share, with a Coriolanus or an Iago, a natural "love of power" over others, but the overall effect of tragedy is to "substitute imaginary sympathy for mere selfishness. It gives us a high and permanent interest, beyond ourselves, in humanity as such." At this point, where imaginative fulfillment culminates in unselfish identification—or, perhaps more accurately, unselfish identification culminates in imaginative fulfillment—Hazlitt's criteria for political and for poetic success become the same. At this point, ideally, both society and a poem achieve an organic unity correlative with the good citizen's and the poet's and the reader's self-integration. Of course, regarding the chances of reaching this ideal, Hazlitt is more sanguine about poetry than about society, although in his own time, he thought, poetry also faced some pretty serious difficulties.[17]

II

As we have seen, Hazlitt's objection to Shelley's and Southey's use of political ideas is that, by beginning with the idea, these poets set up an insuperable barrier to imaginative fulfillment. Wordsworth, too, sometimes stopped short of the kind of imaginative completeness that Hazlitt seeks in literature, but this is because he excessively delighted in "contemplating his own powers" rather than because any set of political ideas intervened. Wordsworth, of course, was no less aware than Hazlitt of the problems that the times imposed on a poet, and if he "contemplated his own powers," it was in order to solve one of the most difficult of these problems. Defining "the triumph of the mechanical philosophy," Basil Willey has noted that by the eighteenth century poets felt that "mythologies, including the Christian, were . . . exploded," that their "truth," as far as it goes, could be stated conceptually (as in the *Essay on Man*), and that they could no longer be used in poetry except as recognized " 'fictions' of proved evocative power and of long association with poetic experience" (as in *The Rape of the Lock*). A

7

major poet, therefore, forced by his concern for truth to deny the old mythologies, had either (like Keats and Shelley, often) to invent a new mythology, although not necessarily discarding all of the old, or (like Wordsworth) to "make poetry out of the direct dealings of his mind and heart with the visible universe . . . ."[18] But if Wordsworth rejected the mythology that had been rejected by scientific thought, he also rejected, as material for poetry, the conceptual world of the new science and (although not fully) the explanatory method of Pope's philosophical poems. In a good many places, including a passage in *The Excursion* (IV, 941-992) which Hazlitt quotes with approval, Wordsworth says that no abstractions should come between the poet and the sensory world which he molds to his thoughts and feelings. Hazlitt gives Wordsworth credit for the "immediate intercourse of [his] imagination with Nature" and his repudiation of the "cold, narrow, lifeless spirit of modern philosophy." "Tintern Abbey" (lines 76-83) shows how "a fine poet . . . describes the effect of the sight of nature on his mind"; and Hazlitt adds praise in what are unquestionably his highest terms: "So the forms of nature . . . stood before the great artists of old. . . ." This is the reason why Wordsworth's "general sentiments and reflections" attain depth, originality, and truth.[19]

The point at which "abstraction" drains the power from Wordsworth's poetry is that at which "vanity" or "egotism" limits his invention to those images, characters, and incidents that are interesting only to himself or, perhaps, other "retired and lonely student[s] of nature. . . ." This is a failure in sympathetic identification. Shakespeare and Milton, through the completeness of their identification with others, gained "a deeper sense . . . of what [is] grand in the objects of nature, or affecting in the events of human life," so that their images, characters, and incidents are meaningful and moving to a large number of readers. Wordsworth's materials, on the other hand, do not touch off such splendid associations. At one extreme, Hazlitt—always empirical—brings the "mysticism" of the Immortality Ode down to earth with a few common-sense observations, although elsewhere he quotes some lines of this poem approvingly. As might be expected, he very often is unsympathetic with the "dim, obscure, and visionary" in Coleridge (although liking parts of "Christabel" and proclaiming "The Ancient Mariner" "a work of genius"); but, as far as Wordsworth is concerned, his usual objection is at the other extreme: to those materials that are ordinary and unpoetic. Vain Wordsworth will "owe nothing but to himself" and therefore abjures "figures," "fantasies," "the gorgeous machinery of mythologic lore," "the splendid colors of poetic diction," "striking subjects," and "remarkable combinations of events" in favor of "the simplest elements of nature and the human mind," "the commonest events and objects," "trifling incidents," "the most insignificant things," and those objects "the most simple and barren of effect." As one might expect, these "objects (whether persons or things)" do not "immediately and irresistibly . . . convey [his feelings] in all their force and depth to others. . . ."[20]

Up to a point, with his emphasis on common experience and general associations, Hazlitt is merely making the same objection to Wordsworth that Jeffrey made in his review of *The Excursion* in November 1814. In his *Encyclopaedia Britannica* article on "Beauty" (1824), which is an expanded version of his May 1811 review of Archibald Alison's *Essays on the Nature and Principles of Taste,* Jeffrey agrees with Alison and others that beauty depends not on a thing itself but on the affections and sympathies that we associate with it. For the *enjoyment* of beauty, therefore, the best taste— which is the awareness of the most beauty—belongs to the person whose affections are so warm and so much exercised that he builds up a multiplicity of pleasurable associations. But Jeffrey is not content with mere subjectivism in art. The *creation* of beauty for others to enjoy requires the poet or artist "to employ only such objects as are the *natural* signs, or the *inseparable* concomitants of emotions, of which the greater part of mankind are susceptible. . . ." If, instead, he obtrudes objects not commonly associated with any interesting impressions, he is guilty of "bad and false" taste. This is Wordsworth's principal defect, resulting, no doubt, from "long habits of seclusion, and an excessive ambition of originality. . . ."[21]

Jeffrey's appeal to the susceptibility of "common minds" does not, regardless of the quality of those minds, set a very sophisticated standard of taste. Art, Jeffrey is saying, offers pleasure like that associated with certain objects in actual life but lacks, or at least makes no use of, an order or truth peculiar to itself. As Wellek points out, "Jeffrey and his models . . . have no criterion to set off enjoyment of a peaceful landscape, or sudden insight into character from experience derived from art objects."[22] Hazlitt frequently invites the same criticism. His highest praise for Shakespeare's characters, for instance, is that we know them as we know real persons or that we can completely identify ourselves with them. As we have seen, he fuses the social and the aesthetic effects of tragedy. He does not, like Coleridge, separate "the Good" and "the Beautiful."

The importance of how a poet combines and organizes his value-charged materials is nevertheless something that Hazlitt was aware of. Although *The Excursion* "excites or recals the same sensations which those who have traversed that wonderful scenery must have felt," Hazlitt adds that "all is left loose and irregular in the rude chaos of aboriginal nature." The cause of this poor construction is egotism: that great fault of the poets of paradox. Wordsworth has merely recorded his own experience—his own sensations and his accompanying feelings and thoughts. The result is not only "nakedness" (of commonplace, undercharged materials) but also "confusion." Wordsworth's structural faults—like the "tendency of [his] mind"—are "the reverse of the dramatic." *The Excursion* lacks what is most important to a dramatic poem—that is, a suitable action or series of actions. Wordsworth would have done better to make the poem completely a "philosophic" one unencumbered by narrative and description which only "hinder the progress and effect of the general reasoning." Evidently Hazlitt thinks that a logical sequence of propositions would be a better unifying principle than broken narrative that "shuns the common 'vantage-grounds of popular story, of striking incident, or fatal catastrophe. . . ." Wordsworth's originality, carried to an egotistical extreme, has hindered him in a way that Scott's lack of originality proved helpful, because, forced to draw on tradition, Scott "selects a story . . . sure to please. . . ." Hazlitt likes these generally exciting incidents for the same reason that he values generally interesting images and characters: that is, as particulars that will excite the reader into imaginative creation. But also Hazlitt thinks of a series of exciting events as central in a poem's structure and, for the best poetry, even indispensable. A painting or a statute can harmonize its varied particulars within the limits of plane or solid geometry, but a poem adds the dimension of time; and to propel the reader's imagination along this axis, a sequence of exciting actions is the most effective means. Unlike the painter or sculptor, the poet must translate "the object [he describes] into some other form, which is the language of metaphor or imagination; as narrative can only interest by a succession of events and a conflict of hopes and fears."[23] Of course Hazlitt admires a number of poems, including a good many of Wordsworth's, which progress through time with little or no narrative; but for Hazlitt, as for Dr. Johnson, the highest sort of invention is narrative and dramatic, with diversified characters clashing in "remarkable combinations of events. . . ." Hazlitt puts a premium on action as providing particulars both individually interesting and collectively propulsive. But he is less interested in a closely knit plot than in a luxuriant texture of feeling. He would have agreed with Matthew

Arnold that "the eternal objects of poetry . . . are actions," that suitable actions "most powerfully appeal to the great human affections," and that a "great" action so dominates a poem with the "feeling of its situations" that it precludes any "detached impressions" or "personal peculiarities."[24]

Broken, undercharged, non-propulsive narrative is of course not the only undramatic sin that Hazlitt traces to Wordsworth's egotism. With "a fastidious antipathy to immediate effect," Wordsworth intrudes into *The Excursion* not only his interpretation of particulars that should not need interpretation but also superfluous particulars that "hang as a dead weight upon the imagination. . . ." There is, furthermore, "no dramatic distinction of character." "The recluse, the pastor, and the pedlar, are three persons in one poet." Hence, because he ascribes the same sort of imaginative coloring of natural objects to all his characters, in this poem and others as well, Wordsworth offends with dramatic impropriety. Hazlitt is willing to accept this coloring or molding as long as Wordsworth does not try to pass it off as some character's rather than his own, but Hazlitt loses faith when Wordsworth makes "pedlars and ploughmen his heroes and . . . interpreters. . . ." Swallowed up by his own feelings, Wordsworth's materials lack variety and contrast. The unity of *The Excursion* lies in "an endless continuity of feeling"—Wordsworth's own—and not in the control of varied materials. The sort of "whole" which Wordsworth "cannot form"—but which Hazlitt prefers—is one that preserves great variety, comprising "all the bustle, machinery, and pantomime of the stage, or of real life . . . ."[25] But the stage and real life are not the same thing, and in an analysis of Hazlitt's criticism both comparisons must be taken into account. Hazlitt rarely lets us forget that he loved the theater—where, of course, he reviewed plays for the *Champion,* the *Examiner,* the *Morning Chronicle,* and *The Times*—but his liking for the dramatic is of one piece with his theory of the imagination. Since imaginative fulfillment depends on a self-denying sympathy, a work of art should break free from self-regard and gain an existence as independent as possible of the purely personal. Invention succeeds as egotism dwindles and as the poet himself appears to drop out altogether, no longer coming between an image, an action, or a character and the reader. Imaginative fulfillment externalizes itself in a form in which the organic and the dramatic are necessary correlatives, duplicating each other as they reach a consummation.

In "Laodamia" (published in 1815 and first mentioned by Hazlitt in 1824 as one of Wordsworth's "later philosophical productions") Hazlitt finds Wordsworth a better craftsman than in *The Excursion.* "Laodamia" is of course a narrative with dialogue, but to explain the poem's structure Hazlitt must obviously look for something other than a succession of lively incidents. ". . . The texture of the thoughts has the smoothness and solidity of marble." In fact, Hazlitt decides that "Laodamia" succeeds in the manner of sculpture or painting, for he applies to the poem a term that he generally reserves for the visual arts: "the ideal." The ideal comprises essential qualities of an object or a person as represented not in the general terms of the understanding but in the particulars seized upon by the imagination in a state of intense feeling. It is "the abstraction of any thing [not from its individuality but] from all the circumstances that weaken its effect, or lessen our admiration of it." It includes, among its conditions, balance, harmony, and repose; consequently it "rejects as much as possible not only the petty, the mean, and disagreeable, but also the agony and violence of passion, the force of contrast, and the extravagance of imagination." Poetry, however, can make good use of these latter qualities; for the poet in translating the object of his imagination into some other form has no choice but a progression through time, for which nothing is better than "a succession of events and a conflict of hopes and fears." Therefore the ideal character, reposing unchanged in harmony, is a handicap to a poet or novelist, providing only "a succession of actions without passion." Hazlitt, as usual, prefers "interesting and dramatic characters" (Shakespeare's), who are "men and not angels." Sculpture and painting must remain the "strong-hold" of the ideal. Yet *in addition to* dynamic progress through varied incidents, the greatest poetry—tragedy—achieves the steady balance of the ideal in "the superiority of character to fortune and circumstances, or the larger scope of thought and feeling thrown into it, that redeems it from the charge of vulgar grossness or physical horrors." Hazlitt finds "permanent tragedy" in the equipoise of "pride of intellect and power . . . confronting and enduring pain" that Milton has given Satan and again in the "feeling of stoical indifference" that Wordsworth achieves in "Laodamia."

> Know, virtue were not virtue, if the joys
> Of sense were able to return as fast
> And surely as they vanish. Earth destroys
> Those raptures duly: *Erebus disdains—*
> *Calm pleasures there abide, majestic pains.*

The speaker, Protesiláus, is obviously an ideal character, but Hazlitt's only adverse comments on this poem are on "some poorness in the diction, and some indistinctness in the images" (both unspecified). ". . . The greater part of [the poem] might be read aloud in Elysium" for the enjoyment of "departed heroes and sages"; and Hazlitt would as soon have written the line "Elysian beauty, melancholy grace" "as have carved a Greek statue."[26] Yet, in the context of Hazlitt's total criticism of Wordsworth and his overall admiration for the dramatic, the structure of "Laodamia"—whereby Wordsworth objectifies his feelings in the static balance of painting and sculpture—scarcely represents a major triumph.

To summarize: the paradoxical, or egotistical, in Wordsworth results not only in materials sometimes lacking general interest, but also in several structural defects: intrusive interpretation and other superfluous interpolations, dramatic impropriety, indistinct characterization, monotony (rather than variety in unity), and actions less than large and controlling. Wordsworth's structural success in "Laodamia" remains of a different order from that which Hazlitt usually admires in poetry.

III

Given these criteria, we may infer why Hazlitt found some of Wordsworth's poems worthy of high praise and why he objected to others. Insofar as Hazlitt deals with specific poems—which is usually in a fragmentary way—the score favors Wordsworth. Howe's index to the *Works* lists thirty-two of Wordsworth's poems by title.[27] Of these, Hazlitt praises eight (six without reservation), favorably quotes six more, expresses disapproval of nine (five of them only for their political sentiments), takes a divided view of one, and quotes or mentions eight more without any clear evaluation—except, of course, that he apparently thought them worth quoting or mentioning. In addition, among those poems of which "it is not possible to speak in terms of too high praise," Hazlitt includes (in his 1818 lecture "On the Living Poets) "several of the Sonnets, and a hundred others of inconceivable beauty, of perfect originality and pathos."[28]

Among the poems that Hazlitt criticizes adversely, *The Excursion* is the only one that he deals with at any length, in the review (appearing in three issues of the *Examiner,* August to October 1814) that I have already discussed. In 1816 he briefly mentions "Simon Lee," along with "ideot boys and mad mothers," to suggest the meanness of Wordsworth's materials. This also seems to be his objection, in 1821, to "The Leech-gatherer," although, like other critics from Coleridge on, he greatly admired parts of this poem; and in 1817, as we have seen, he found fault with the "mysticism" in the Immortality Ode. In the remaining poems in this group—"Gipsies," the sonnet "November, 1813," the Thanksgiving Ode, and the sonnets on Schill and Hofer—Hazlitt finds evidence of Wordsworth's apostasy and is characteristically scornful of such support for the ruling class and "legitimacy."[29] His comments on these five poems all follow Napoleon's defeat at Waterloo in June 1815 and, except for one mention of the Hofer and Schill sonnets in 1828 (when Hazlitt was working on his *Life of Napoleon*), they fall within Hazlitt's most active period as a political writer (from his reply to "Vetus" in November 1813 to the publication of *Political Essays* in 1819).

This period was marked by the restoration of the Bourbons abroad and by further denials of civil liberty in England: by hard times, riots, and countermeasures leading to the brutality and slaughter at Peterloo. Although, as Talfourd reports, Hazlitt was "staggered under the blow" of Napoleon's defeat, the succeeding months and years find him as resolute as ever, in a time when such resolution was far from safe, in attacking the divine right of kings, the Congress of Vienna, the hanging of John Cashman for his part in the Spa-Fields riot, the reduction of the Poor Rates, Castlereagh, Canning, Malthus, Gifford, and, on political grounds, his one-time friends and fellow-revolutionaries Coleridge, Wordsworth, and Southey. If these attacks seem severe, we must recall the political climate in which Wordsworth, in his Thanksgiving Ode (1816), could praise an aggressive Deity for his "pure intent" worked out in "Man—arrayed for mutual slaughter" and Southey could write in 1817: "We are in danger of an insurrection of the Yahoos:—it is the fault of the governments that such a cast should exist in the midst of civilized society, but till the breed can be mended it must be curbed, & that too with a strong hand."[30] It was during this period that the Tory periodicals, the *Quarterly* and *Blackwood's,* responded to Hazlitt's attack on the government with vicious and libelous abuse and that, after Hazlitt's review of *The Excursion,* Wordsworth took some pains to spread his report of an incident, evidently some sexual adventure of Hazlitt's, that had taken place near Keswick in 1803. Wordsworth reported the matter in conversations with Lamb (1814) and Crabb Robinson (1815); and writing to John Scott on 11 June 1816, in a passage omitted from *The Letters of William and Dorothy Wordsworth,* Wordsworth mentioned that he had told Haydon of the 1803 incident and concluded that Hazlitt is "a man of low propensities, & of bad heart. . . . His sensations are too corrupt to allow him to understand my Poetry—though his ingenuity might enable him so to write as if he knew something about it." In the 7 April 1817 letter already quoted (p. 2 above) Wordsworth urged Haydon "not to associate with the Fellow, he is not a

proper person to be admitted into respectable society, being the most perverse and malevolent Creature that ill luck has ever thrown in my way.
Avoid him—hic niger est—And this, I understand, is the general opinion
wherever he is known in London."[31] One can understand the relish with
which, in his lecture "On the Living Poets" (1818), Hazlitt said that Wordsworth's

egotism is in some respects a madness. . . . He hates all science and all art;
he hates chemistry, he hates conchology; he hates Voltaire; he hates Sir Isaac
Newton; he hates wisdom; he hates wit; he hates metaphysics, which he says
are unintelligible, and yet he would be thought to understand them; he hates
prose; he hates all poetry but his own; he hates the dialogues in Shakespeare;
he hates music, dancing, and painting; he hates Rubens, he hates Rembrandt;
he hates Raphael, he hates Titian; he hates Vandyke; he hates the antique;
he hates the Apollo Belvidere; he hates the Venus of Medicis. This is
the reason that so few people take an interest in his writings, because he takes
an interest in nothing that others do!

Yet it is in this same lecture that Hazlitt has only the highest praise for more
than a "hundred" of Wordsworth's poems; and seven years later, in *The
Spirit of the Age,* where Hazlitt makes his usual high evaluation of much
of Wordsworth's poetry but with particular appreciation of "his later philosophic productions," Hazlitt refers to his earlier list of Wordsworth's hates
as "mere epigrams and *jeux-d'esprit,* as far from truth as they are free from
malice. . . ."[32]

In "The Thorn," the "Mad Mother" ["Her eyes are wild"], and "The
Complaint of a Poor Indian Woman" [*sic*], Hazlitt found, when Coleridge
read these poems aloud to him in January 1798, "that deeper power and
pathos which have since been acknowledged . . . as the characteristics of [the]
author. . . ." At least this is the discovery that Hazlitt affirmed in "My First
Acquaintance with Poets" (1823). In 1818 he again listed the "Complaint"
among those others of Wordsworth's poems of which "it is not possible to
speak in terms of too high praise": "Hart-Leap Well," "The Banks of the
Wye" ["Tintern Abbey"], "The Reverie of Poor Susan," parts of "The
Leech-gatherer," "To a Cuckoo [*sic*], and "To a Daisy" [*sic*] (which may
be any of the three poems Wordsworth called "To the Daisy" but which,
because all the other poems referred to in "On the Living Poets" had been
published by 1807, is probably one of the two poems of this title that appeared
in the 1807 edition, although the one in the 1815 edition cannot be ruled
out). "Hart-Leap Well" seems to be Hazlitt's favorite, with "Laodamia"
later becoming a close competitor.[33]

In all of these, we may infer, Hazlitt discovered not only profound thoughts and sentiments but also a satisfactory degree of "fanciful invention." Five of these poems—"The Thorn," "Her eyes were wild," "The Complaint," "Hart-Leap Well," and "Laodamia"—are dramatic in that each deals with a tense, crucial situation and that the speakers, except in a very minor way in "Hart-Leap Well," are not the poet himself; all five have a distinct narrative element; and all have vivid and splendid or awesome imagery. Apparently—in 1798 and again in 1823—Hazlitt did not consider "The Thorn" and "Her eyes were wild" irreparably damaged by psychotic mothers or "a little muddy pond." In "Hart-Leap Well" Wordsworth, it seems, has found a suitable story—somewhat like Scott's material—to dramatize the thought and sentiment expressed in the last stanza (with what, according to Hazlitt's standards, one might consider an excess of interpretation and, indeed, interpretation that is not adequately prepared for dramatically). Hazlitt's reasons for admiring "Laodamia" have already been examined. The parts of "The Leech-gatherer" that pleased Hazlitt can only be guessed at: perhaps he felt, in the measured cheerfulness of the old man, something of the reposeful "ideal" that he discovered in "Laodamia";[34] probably he liked the sentiment and some of the imagery, but not the inelegant details ("muddy water" again). The old man is scarcely of lower station than the "poor Indian woman" (although, a local product, he may seem more commonplace), but his situation is less immediately dramatic, the poem's narrative interest is slight, and characterization remains indistinct (as Charles Williams notes, the Leech-gatherer seems to be "the impersonated thought of some other state of being, which the acceptance of the noble doctrine it teaches leaves in itself unexplored").[35]

In "Tintern Abbey," which was written later than any other poem in the first edition of *Lyrical Ballads,* F. W. Bateson points out that "Wordsworth [practically for the first time] speaks the language that he was afterwards to speak in prose and in verse. . . . With its long sentences, its involved grammar and its polysyllabic vocabulary it was a form of discourse that abandoned all pretense to being the poetry of the people."[36] In another respect, however—in its direct molding of sensory experience to the poet's feelings—it is still paradoxical, and it is for this quality that Hazlitt especially admires the poem and places Wordsworth in "a totally distinct class of excellence." Wordsworth has become openly autobiographical, and the analysis of his own mental processes has become as important as the details of external nature.[37] But of course the poem escapes the excesses of paradox: in ascribing these sensations, thoughts, and feelings to himself and Dorothy, Wordsworth does not commit any dramatic impropriety; more than in the Immortality Ode he keeps his consolation for the loss of youth's "dizzy raptures" within empirical (if not entirely logical) limits; and, to be sure, no mud puddles or molehills devalue the banks of the Wye as material for poetry.

We may only infer Hazlitt's reasons for mentioning the remaining three poems favorably; and for lack of specific evidence, these inferences must be brief. "The Reverie of Poor Susan," although not published until 1800, was written before "Tintern Abbey" and is a kind of preliminary sketch for it. It avoids the first person; and its concrete particulars are appropriate to the character (therefore "dramatic" and not merely "picturesque"). The poem has a clear chronological structure, with its parts neatly describing successive stages of the process of association: the initiating bird song, the delightful recall of pleasing images, and their subsequent fading away. "To the Cuckoo" is a first-person lyric with a good deal of generally appealing concrete detail; the imagery is given texture by the basic metaphor (the bird is a "Voice" suggesting "an unsubstantial, faery" world). A very similar case could be made for the 1807 daisy poem beginning "In youth from rock to rock," while the other daisy poem of that year, beginning "Bright Flower," although less concrete is closely structured and is a good example of unmuddied Nature imaginatively molded to express profound sentiments.

IV

In an article on "Hazlitt's Preference for Tragedy" (*PMLA*, LXXI [1956], 1042-51) I wrote that Hazlitt's practical criticism is in some respects better than his theory. This might also be said about his favorite thesis that imaginative activity has steadily declined since Shakespeare and Milton; for this thesis forced him to put the poetry of paradox at the bottom of his scale, whereas his evaluation of Wordsworth's individual poems is usually a high one. Despite personal and political animosity, Hazlitt recognized the imaginative power of Wordsworth's "immediate intercourse" with sensory nature, his consequent kinship with "the great artists of old," and his unique excellence in his own time.

But this imaginative excellence, Hazlitt believes, has been pulled up short of fulfillment, and therefore lacks the dramatic invention that the greatest poetry requires. If Hazlitt's estimate of Wordsworth is high, it is also discriminating. Wordsworth shares the fault that, in general at least, gives his contemporaries the lowest place on Hazlitt's scale. Hazlitt's case against contemporary poetry rests on the various kinds of egotism that perverted reason or—what is more important to Hazlitt—blocked the imagination. He objects to the "literary Jacobinism" of Landor and Southey, to the intrusion of political ideas by Shelley and Godwin and of metaphysics by Coleridge, to Wordsworth's choice of materials remote from general experience and interest, and to the structural defects of paradox: interpretation, needless interpolation, dramatic impropriety, lack of variety, and slightness of action. Hazlitt nevertheless takes account of Wordsworth's "ideal" but undramatic structure in "Laodamia." Hazlitt's ideas of structure are obviously less sophisticated and less comprehensive than those that have become current in this century, but they are sound and fundamental.

Hazlitt is always searching literature for the kind of truth that duplicates nature; but, at the same time, his respect for the truth of nature (imaginatively molded, but undistorted by the merely personal) leads to his high regard for the kind of poetry that has broken free from the poet himself. This freedom is most complete when the structure is most completely dramatic. There is nothing contradictory in this emphasis on both the truth of nature and poetic structure. The poet's imagination can embrace the truth of nature only when unhampered by any sort of egotism, for truth requires complete self-fulfillment—intellectual, emotional, and moral—and, if the process of association leading to this fulfillment is blocked by preconceived ideas or other forms of self-regard, the highest truth will not be attained. Thus the process of imagination and artistic creation proceeds simultaneously toward two goals, each dependent on the other: the completeness of self-fulfillment and its counterpart in organic yet objective form wherein "profound sentiments" are realized in images, characters, and incidents of the most pleasing and striking kind. Only then is the poet's invention rich enough to embody profound sentiments.

Nor is there any inconsistency between Hazlitt's revolutionary political doctrine and his repudiation of this doctrine as material for poetry. *Any* doctrine, *egotistically* insisted on, aborts the imaginative completeness that Hazlitt makes the basis of both aesthetic and political achievement, a process that integrates the individual—and, ideally, society—emotionally, intellectually, and morally. Successful literature, therefore, cannot help being politically and socially useful, and there can be no basic conflict between humanitarian goals and poetic achievement. If Hazlitt is guilty of a paradox, it is one that his job as a political writer made difficult to avoid, for the urgency of writing on current issues puts negative capability to a bitter test. Of course, negative capability is a condition of imaginative writing only; but Hazlitt's political essays are rarely, if ever, addressed to consequitive reasoners. Since, to combat the "cold, philosophic indifference" of his opponents,[38] Hazlitt exploits all the resources of literature, his political writings become imaginative works into which he rushes with ideas as demonstratively preconceived as Shelley's and Southey's.

Yet, as positive as Hazlitt may be on basic principles, almost the whole body of his political writing aims at the negation of political actions that he thought would further restrict the people's rights. He opposed Poor-Law reform, for instance, because—inadequate as the Poor Laws were—he believed that in the current political atmosphere of selfishness and greed any legislative action would hurt the working classes more than it would help them. Hazlitt is more like Arnold than a first glance might suggest. Before right was ready, he thought, he could do no more in a practical way than to stand off further wrongs. Politically as well as aesthetically, he urges disinterestedness: the sympathetic identification that is needed for imaginative fulfillment. This is clear in Hazlitt's political writings. Among his critical essays it is clearest in his criticism of Wordsworth, the chief poet of paradox.

NOTES

1. "On Dryden and Pope" and "On the Living Poets," *Lectures on the English Poets,* in *The Complete Works of William Hazlitt,* ed. P. P. Howe (London, 1930-34), V, 82-83, 161-162.

2. "On the Living Poets," p. 162.

3. Letter dated 7 April 1817, *The Letters of William and Dorothy Wordsworth,* ed. E. de Selincourt (Oxford, 1937), II, 781; Charles Whibley, "Hazlitt v. 'Blackwood's Magazine,'" *Blackwood's Magazine,* CCIV (1918), 388-398.

4. "The Periodical Press," *Contributions to the Edinburgh Review,* in *Works,* XVI, 233. In an invaluable book published since this article was completed (*William Hazlitt,* Cambridge, Mass., 1962, pp. 340-355 *et passim*), Herschel Baker shows that Hazlitt's rancorous and tiresome attacks on Wordsworth, Coleridge, and Southey anticipate the abuse Hazlitt himself later received in the *Quarterly* and *Blackwood's.* But Hazlitt's critical principles will usually account for his appraisal of most of these poets' poems. Mr. Baker adds that even when, in his review of *The Excursion,* Hazlitt apparently decided "to treat a serious if imperfect work of art with the dignity it deserved . . . his criticism merges into politics." But, if the part of this review dealing with Wordsworth's politics were omitted, Hazlitt's evaluation of the poem, and his reasons for it, would remain the same.

5. "Character of Mr. Wordsworth's New Poem, The Excursion," *Works,* XIX, 11 (a revised version of this essay appears in *The Round Table,* in *Works,* IV, 112-125); René Wellek, *A History of Modern Criticism: 1750-1950,* Part II, *The Romantic Age* (New Haven, 1955), p. 210; "On the Intellectual Character of the Late William Hazlitt," *Critical and Miscellaneous Writings of T. Noon Talfourd* (Philadelphia, 1852), p. 129 (*The Examiner,* 14 and 21 Oct. and 4 Nov. 1832, pp. 661-662, 678, 708-709). See also T. N. Talfourd, *Memoirs of Charles Lamb* (London, 1892), p. 180.

6. "On the Living Poets," pp. 162-163; "Lord Byron" and "Mr. Southey," *The Spirit of the Age,* in *Works,* XI, 71, 77, 80; "On Effeminacy of Character," *Table-Talk,* in *Works,* VIII, 255; "Coleridge's Literary Life," "Landor's Imaginary Conversations," and "Shelley's Posthumous Poems," *Contributions to the Edinburgh Review,* pp. 137-138, 240-241, 244, 267.

7. "On Poetry in General" and "On Shakspeare and Milton," *Lectures on the English Poets,* pp. 3-6, 53-54, 58-59; "On Reason and Imagination," *The Plain Speaker,* in *Works,* XII, 51; "On Genius and Common Sense," *Table-Talk,* pp. 35, 40-41. See also J. M. Bullitt, "Hazlitt and the Romantic Conception of the Imagination," *PQ,* XXIV (1945), 343-361; W. J. Bate, *Criticism: The Major Texts* (New York, 1952), pp. 281-292; and my article "Hazlitt's Preference for Tragedy," *PMLA,* LXXI (1956), 1042-51.

8. "On Gusto," *The Round Table,* p. 77.

9. "Character of . . . The Excursion," pp. 18-19.

10. "Why the Arts Are Not Progressive," *The Round Table,* pp. 160-164; "The Drama: No. IV," *Works,* XVIII, 304-305; "On Poetry in General," pp. 9-10.

11. "Character of . . . The Excursion," pp. 15-17.

12. "Shelley's Posthumous Poems," *Contributions to the Edinburgh Review,* pp. 265, 269; "Mr. Southey" and "Mr. Coleridge," *The Spirit of the Age,* pp. 30, 79.

13. "Character of . . . The Excursion," p. 16; "The Drama: No. IV," pp. 308-309; Keats's letters dated 22 Nov. 1817, 27 (?) Dec. 1817, about 27 Oct. 1818, and 19 March 1819, *The Letters of John Keats 1814-1821,* ed. H. E. Rollins (Cambridge, Mass., 1958), I, 184-185, 193-194, 388-390; II, 79-80. See also Lionel Trilling, ed., *The Selected Letters of John Keats* (Garden City, N. Y., 1956), pp. 27-28.

14. *The Major English Romantic Poets: A Symposium in Reappraisal,* ed. C. D. Thorpe *et al.* (Carbondale, Ill., 1957), pp. 237-238; "On Poetry in General," p. 6.

15. "Coriolanus," *A View of the English Stage,* in *Works,* V, 347-348; or "Coriolanus," *Characters of Shakespear's Plays,* in *Works,* IV, 214-215; "Illustrations of 'The Times' Newspaper," *Political Essays,* in *Works,* VII, 142.

16. "Project for a New Theory of Civil and Criminal Legislation," *Works,* XIX, 303-305; *An Essay on the Principles of Human Action,* in *Works,* I, 1, 9-10, *et passim;* "What is the People?" *Political Essays,* pp. 267-270; "On Reason and Imagination," *The Plain Speaker,* in *Works,* XII, 44-55. Cf., for similarities and possible indebtedness, Rousseau, *The Social Contract,* Book I, ch. viii; Book II, ch. vii; Book IV, ch. ii, iii.

17. "On Poetry in General," pp. 5-8; "Othello" and "Lear," *Characters of Shakespear's Plays,* pp. 200, 205, 271-272; "Illustrations of 'The Times' Newspaper," pp. 142-145. See also my article "Hazlitt's Preference for Tragedy" (see note 7) and my reply to S. Barnet, "More on Hazlitt's Preference for Tragedy," *PMLA,* LXXIII (1958), 444-445.

18. "Character of . . . The Excursion," pp. 15-16; Basil Willey, *The Seventeenth Century Background* (London, 1934), pp. 296-297.

19. "Character of . . . The Excursion," pp. 11-14; "On Application to Study," *The Plain Speaker,* pp. 59-60.

20. "Mr. Wordsworth," pp. 86-89; "On Shakspeare and Milton," pp. 47, 53; "Romeo and Juliet," *Characters of Shakespear's Plays,* p. 250; "On Thomson and Cowper," *Lectures on the English Poets,* p. 103; "Mr. Coleridge's Christabel," *Works,* XIX, 33-34; "Mr. Coleridge," *The Spirit of the Age,* pp. 34-35; "Coleridge's Lay Sermon" and "Coleridge's Literary Life," *Contributions to the Edinburgh Review,* pp. 101, 137; "Character of . . . The Excursion," pp. 9-10, 19.

21. Francis Jeffrey, *Contributions to the Edinburgh Review* (New York, 1869), pp. 35, 38-39, 458.

22. Pp. 114-115.

23. "Character of . . . The Excursion," pp. 9-12; "On the Living Poets," pp. 154-154; "The Ideal," *Works,* XX, 305.

24. "Dedication to Shakespear Illustrated," *The Works of Samuel Johnson* (London, 1788), XIV, 477-478; 'Preface to the First Edition of *Poems* (1853)," *The Complete Prose Works of Matthew Arnold,* ed. R. H. Super (Ann Arbor, 1960), I, 3-6. See also "On the English Novelists" and "On the Works of Hogarth," *Lectures on the English Comic Writers,* in *Works,* VI, 128, 142; "American Literature—Dr. Channing" and "Mr. Godwin," *Contributions to the Edinburgh Review,* pp. 320, 395; and "Dunlop's History of Fiction" in the Waller and Glover edition of Hazlitt's *Works* (London, 1904), X, 5, 11, 17, although the attribution of this essay to Hazlitt is rejected by Howe (XVI, 420).

25. "Character of . . . The Excursion," pp. 11-13, 20; "On the Living Poets," p. 156; "Mr. Wordsworth," p. 92. See also "Sismondi's Literature of the South," *Contributions to the Edinburgh Review,* pp. 41-43, 54.

26. "Mr. Wordsworth," p. 90; "The Ideal," pp. 302-306; "On the Picturesque and Ideal," *Table-Talk,* pp. 317-321; "Landor's Imaginary Conversations," p. 253; "Old English Writers and Speakers," *The Plain Speaker,* p. 320.

27. This count assumes that "The Banks of the Wye" ("On the Living Poets," p. 156) is

"Tintern Abbey," which Hazlitt elsewhere praises under its usual title (note 20 above). Hazlitt also mentions, as one of his favorites, a poem not known to be by Wordsworth, "Lines on a Picture by Claude Lorraine." Martha Hale Shackford conjectures that this title is "probably a mistake for Southey's *On a Landscape by Gaspar Poussin* (1797)" (*Wordsworth's Interest in Painters and Pictures,* Wellesley, Mass., 1945, p. 51). Hazlitt includes these "Lines," along with "Laodamia" (1815), among Wordsworth's "later philosophic productions" ("Mr. Wordsworth," p. 90). I have also assumed, with Howe, that "The Complaint" mentioned in "On the Living Poets" (p. 156) is "The Complaint of a Forsaken Indian Woman" (also admired in "My First Acquaintance with Poets") and not "A Complaint" ("There is a change").

28. "On the Living Poets," p. 156.
29. "The Lay of the Laureate" and "Illustrations of 'The Times' Newspaper," *Political Essays,* in *Works,* VII, 96 n., 133, 144; "On Swift, Young, Gray, Collins, etc.," and "On the Living Poets," *Lectures on the English Poets,* pp. 122, 156; "On Consistency of Opinion," *Works,* XVII, 25; "On Manner," *The Round Table,* pp. 45-46, n., "Comus" and "Coriolanus," *A View of the English Stage,* pp. 233 n., 348; *Letter to William Gifford,* in *Works,* IX, 39; "Mr. Landor's Imaginary Conversations," *Works,* XIX, 108; "The Press . . . ," *Works,* XIX, 204.
30. Talfourd, *Memoirs of Charles Lamb,* p. 189; Southey's letter dated 13 March 1817, quoted in P. P. Howe, *The Life of William Hazlitt* (Penguin Books, 1949), p. 230. See also C. C. Southey (ed.), *The Life and Correspondence of Robert Southey* (London, 1850), IV, 239-240, 243-244, 247-248, 295-296; Catherine M. Maclean, *Born under Saturn* (New York, 1944), pp. 326 ff.
31. Howe, *Life,* pp. 99-101; Maclean, pp. 360, 600 n., *The Times Literary Supplement,* No. 2082 (27 Dec. 1941), p. 660; Wordsworth, *Letters,* II, 746-749, 781-782.
32. "On the Living Poets," pp. 163-164; "Mr. Wordsworth," pp. 90, 94.
33. "My First Acquaintance with Poets," *Works,* XVII, 117; "On the Living Poets," pp. 156-161; 'On the Character of Rousseau," *The Round Table,* p. 92; "Character of . . . The Excursion," p. 24. In addition, Hazlitt quotes, with approval of the sentiments therein, lines from "The Borderers," "Expostulation and Reply," "The Fountain," "My heart leaps up," "Personal Talk," and "The world is too much with us."
34. Cf. John Jones, *The Egotistical Sublime* (London, 1954), pp. 60-64.
35. Charles Williams, *The English Poetic Mind* (Oxford, 1932), p. 160.
36. *Wordsworth—A Reinterpretation,* 2d ed. (London, 1956), pp. 142-143.
37. See *ibid.,* p. 140.
38. *Reply to the Essay on Population,* in *Works,* I, 185-186.

Browning's Use of Historical Sources in *Strafford*

by Harold Orel

The obstinacy with which Robert Browning pursued an unsuccessful play-writing career, even at some expense to his personal fortune, is a remarkable aspect of his life. His plays failed to attract large audiences. Some of them were not produced during his lifetime, and *Luria*—so far as I know—has never been performed. *A Soul's Tragedy,* though not meant for the stage, was cast in the form of a play, and the London Stage Society's production of it in 1904 confirmed the dismal general impression of the poet's "dramas." Why, then, did Browning persist for so long?

When Browning responded to William Charles Macready's invitation to write a play and keep the actor-producer from going to America,[1] he was undoubtedly hoping to elevate the dreary standards of early nineteenth-century drama. A clash in personalities soon indicated to Macready that Browning was ignorant of, and perhaps unsympathetic toward, the available resources and needs of the contemporary stage.[2] Browning, like Tennyson (who, later in the century, entertained an ambition to supplement Shakespeare's cycle of historical plays), never learned to write plays that would satisfy both his own standards as a poet and the tastes of Victorian audiences.

Later admirers of Browning have ignored his plays[3] in favor of his narrative, dramatic, and lyric poems. For Browning, a failure to do as much as he thought possible to do was frustrating enough; but he never knew objectively how well he had done. His wife's evaluations of the worth of his plays influenced him greatly; but she never saw their virtues in quite the same way as he did, and, in general, she did not approve of his play-writing.

The aim of this paper is to look more closely at *Strafford,* the first of Browning's seven essays at conventional dramatic form (five dramas and two "closet pieces" over a ten-year period), and in some ways the most interesting experiment he ever carried through. Macready, who at first doubted that it would be successful, worked hard to stage it. During the final rehearsals his hopes rose higher than the event justified; but the play was not a disaster, and Macready's respectable production turned it into a moderate, and limited, success. His editorial work on subsequent plays submitted to him by Browning was more rough-shod, even brutal, and *Strafford* as a text is certainly closer to what Browning intended than *A Blot in the 'Scutcheon,* which Macready produced after proposing cuts that ran to approximately 25 per cent of the play, and certainly a better play than *The Return of the*

Druses, which Macready, out of patience, finally refused to produce. If any of Browning's plays deserves study, it is *Strafford.*

Thomas Wentworth, Earl of Strafford, was an English historical figure of some complexity, even ambiguity, who moved with a dignified and noble eloquence toward his premature death. Browning depended for most of his facts on John Forster's *Life,* which appeared in 1836 as Volume II of *Lives of Eminent British Statesmen* in *The Cabinet Cyclopaedia.* F. J. Furnivall claimed, in the 1892 reprint published under the auspices of the London Browning Society, that Browning had contributed a great deal to the writing of Forster's *Life;* but William Clyde DeVane doubts, with some justice, that Browning's collaboration was quite so extensive.[4] Browning probably contributed his help more in the way of interpretations than in the way of actual phraseology, and most likely after all the materials had been collected. These materials were to be found in the article in *Biographia Britannica;* in the life in Macdiarmid's *British Statesmen;* in Sir George Radcliffe's memoir; and in the selection from Strafford's letters published by Dr. Knowler in 1739. Indeed, as the historian C. H. Firth remarked in the London Browning Society reprint, a biographer of Strafford in 1836 had a larger amount of information at his disposal than in the case of any other statesman of the seventeenth century.

What Browning wrote of the history cannot be known at this late date. Furnivall's assumption that Browning ought to have most of the credit depends, in part, on remarks that the poet made to him on three separate occasions; and in part on a feeling that certain passages are in the poet's idiom. But Furnivall admits that he never inquired directly as to just how much Browning contributed. We do know that Forster made the full collections and extracts, and since the stage at which the poet was asked to assume the final editing remains unspecified, the reprinting of Forster's biographical sketch as *Robert Browning's Prose Life of Strafford* seems unwarranted.

Firth's severe strictures against Browning as historian have remained unchallenged for some seven decades. Forster's illness certainly contributed to the haste and inadequacy of the memoir, and the evidence, as Firth remarked, was "in many respects defective."[5] Historians might well object to a point of view that interpreted Strafford's motives on the basis of two centuries of hindsight. After all, 1836 is not 1632, and Strafford was not a party man; in brief, his character did not drastically change when he deserted the popular party, and his conduct is only superficially explained by such phrases as "the development of the aristocratic principle" and "the intensity of the aristocratic principle." Firth's censure is based upon the belief that Strafford regarded as compatible "the liberties of the people and the prerogative of the Crown"[6] and that the King (rather than Parliament) would be the natural ally of a reformer.

But the indictment does not end there. Browning's sketchy knowledge of the first half of the seventeenth century, and the meager documentation for Strafford's earlier career, contributed to some misleading chiaroscuro. The poet, argues Firth, unfairly minimized the value of Wentworth's work in Ireland; the restoration of order, the establishment of a reign of impartial justice, and the increase of material prosperity were all accomplished under Strafford's reign, even if the minister used force freely and argued that the end justified the means. Browning failed to consult the Hardwicke State Papers, the Clarendon State Papers, and Rushworth for the information he needed about the fourteen months that followed Strafford's return to England (September 22, 1639). He attributed to Strafford several mistresses—Lady Carlisle, Lady Carnarvon, and Lady Loftus—on "very insufficient evidence," and, in the case of Lady Carnarvon, "entirely . . . on a confusion of names."[7] He criticized Strafford's behavior toward his third wife, but, Firth remarks, nobody really knows much about the circumstances of the marriage.

Now these are serious charges, even though, as I have sought to show, Browning's degree of culpability is conjectural, and even though, as I personally believe, Firth's faith in the objectivity of "true history" leads one to inquire whether the phrase is not an oxymoron. It may well be impossible to remain unaffected by the assumptions of one's own age, despite the fact that one may recognize and deplore them. But Browning's dilemma is worth considering in more detail, for, even when we grant the literary and dramatic failings of *Strafford,* the charge that the events of the play constitute a faulty reading of history, and are based upon a similarly faulty historical memoir, will not bear up under examination.

Strafford as a play differs in several significant respects from the memoir that both Forster and Browning wrote. (Firth acknowledged the existence of these differences, but failed to stress their dramatic usefulness to Browning.) For example, Strafford in the memoir is not mentioned as intending to accuse Pym and his associates of maintaining clandestine relations with the rebels, and encouraging them to bring a Scottish army into England; in the play the accusation becomes an effective moment in Act III, Scene ii. Strafford's trial is unusual (in history) because of the change of procedure from impeachment to attainder; Firth argues that the importance of this change is "inadequately appreciated" by Browning and that the facts are not correctly told; but the speeches of Vane and Pym in Act IV, Scene ii, emphasize the true meaning of the change. Vane, for example, denounces the new course of action:

> Consider, Pym!
> Confront your Bill, your own Bill: what is it?
> You cannot catch the Earl on any charge,—
> No man will say the law has hold of him
> On any charge; and therefore you resolve
> To take the general sense on his desert,
> As though no law existed, and we met
> To found one. You refer to Parliament
> To speak its thought upon the abortive mass
> Of half-borne-out assertions, dubious hints
> Hereafter to be cleared, distortions—ay,
> And wild inventions. Every man is saved
> The task of fixing any single charge
> On Strafford: he has but to see in him
> The enemy of England.[8]

Pym's defense, belligerently given, provides a measure of the passions which Strafford's conduct under the King's protection stirred up:

> By this, we roll the clouds away
> Of precedent and custom, and at once
> Bid the great beacon-light God sets in all,
> The conscience of each bosom, shine upon
> The guilt of Strafford: each man lay his hand
> Upon his breast, and judge![9]

A reader may well ask whether Strafford's sense of betrayal, after receipt of the news that the King had signed the Bill, is communicated by the historically probable, "My body is theirs, but my soul is God's. There is little trust in man; God may yet, if it please him, deliver me," or the poetically brilliant,

> Put not your trust
> In princes, neither in the sons of men,
> In whom is no salvation![10]

In at least one case, Firth's literal reading of the primary source seems less convincing than the interpretation provided by either the memoir or the play. During the trial Pym's peroration in defense of the law which was to result in Strafford's condemnation concluded with the statement, "There are marks enough to trace this law to the very original of this kingdom; and if it hath not been put in execution, as he allegeth, this 240 years, it was not for want of a law, but that all that time hath not bred a man bold enough to commit such crimes as these!" At this moment, according to Forster and Browning (quoting Baillie), "Strafford had been closely and earnestly watching Pym, when the latter, suddenly turning, met the fixed and wasted features of his early associate. A rush of other feelings crowding into that look for a moment dispossessed him. 'His papers he looked on,' says Baillie, 'but they could not help him to a point or two, so he behooved to pass them.' But a moment, and Pym's eloquence and dignified command returned." Browning recaptures this moment in Act IV, Scene ii, when the spectators of the trial, in a passage adjoining Westminster Hall, are startled by Pym's momentary faltering at the moment he beholds Strafford's face:

> There!
> What ails him? No—he rallies, see—goes on,
> And Strafford smiles. Strange![11]

Firth admits that the incident is dramatic, but argues that all the authorities say is, that during Pym's answer to Strafford's defense his memory for a moment failed him.[12] However, there is no real evidence for or against this "striking incident," and Browning's interpretation is both imaginative and plausible.

The major value of Firth's analysis is that it notes the existence of a real willingness on Browning's part to go along with the judgment of Strafford's contemporaries: to judge the statesman with too great harshness, but to treat the personal characteristics and the private life with great fairness (though even here, Firth hastens to add, there are occasional errors and omissions in his sketch). The major defect is that it unsympathetically rejects any reading of the data that the primary sources do not explicitly provide; as a young historian in his thirty-fifth year, Firth had not yet developed the broader perspective of his later studies of the Protectorate. That another view of Browning's achievement can be held may be seen in R. S. Gardiner's statement that this is a poet's conception of Strafford's life: "Yes, it makes mistakes in facts and dates, but it has got the man—in the main."[13]

For the moment, let us suspend judgment on the somewhat arid question whether Strafford is historically convincing, and investigate the means by which Browning established the nature and intensity of Parliament's opposition to Strafford.

The case against Strafford was a complicated one. He was the King's man, and as such represented the principle of autocratic whim which could not be directly touched by those who most hated it. Since Charles was notoriously unstable in his policies, and could be swayed by those near him who urged their policies with greatest eloquence, revenge against the royal power could be taken only by a crippling blow delivered against his favorite. That Charles failed to understand the true direction of Parliament's hatred when he agreed to allow Parliament to strike down his loyal minister proved one of the final ironies of his unhappy career.

But Strafford personally was a difficult man to love. Sir Henry Vane—who had ample cause not to admire him—cited several reasons why his adversary had become dangerous and untrustworthy in the decade since he last sat with the Faction.

> . . . when I think on all that's past
> Since that man left us, how his single arm
> Rolled the advancing good of England back
> And set the woeful past up in its place,
> Exalting Dagon where the Ark should be,—
> How that man has made firm the fickle King
> (Hampden, I will speak out!)—in aught he feared
> To venture on before; taught tyranny
> Her dismal trade, the use of all her tools,
> To ply the scourge yet screw the gag so close
> That strangled agony bleeds mute to death—
> How he turns Ireland to a private stage
> For training infant villainies, new ways
> Of wringing treasure out of tears and blood . . . .
>   (I, i)[14]

Vane's argument was a compelling one; no man knew what Wentworth dared, what the King was capable of doing now that his favorite had returned from Ireland (where he had been carrying out his policy of Thorough), or how the unpopular policies of Hamilton, Cottington, and Laud might yet—in Rudyard's words—"be longed-for back again."

Hence, the first of the four problems that Browning had to resolve before *Strafford* could become dramatically viable may be stated thus: *the issues responsible for the Civil War were too complicated, and the number of years involved too great, for any balanced review of the historical evidence.* Quite apart from the question of whether Macready's audience wanted such a review in the theatre, the two hours' traffic of the stage made it necessary for him to create in John Pym Strafford's fearsome antagonist, and, as a consequence, to oversimplify or ignore such issues as the Petition of Right; the payment of ship-money; the complicated relationship of Scotland to both the Crown and the Faction; the degree to which Wentworth personally profited from the conversion of Ireland to an Aceldama (although Lady Carlisle dared to mention the popular unrest over his profit in the Customs, I, ii); the twelve subsidies which the King demanded; the contents of the indictment drawn up against the Earl; and the damning notes which Vane sent to Pym, sealing Strafford's fate. This concentration on personality has recently been deplored by H. B. Charlton, and the essay in which Charlton makes his case against Browning's lack of interest in social institutions and social organization is a powerful one.[15] Nevertheless, if choice had to be made and some elements stressed at the expense of others, Pym's fanatical determination to crush Strafford is surely the most dramatic single element Browning could have seized upon.

Pym's greatness is never in question, from the moment he announces to his followers at the house near Whitehall:

> Heaven grows dark above:
> Let's snatch one moment ere the thunder fall,
> To say how well the English spirit comes out
> Beneath it! (I, i)[16]

to the final terrible confrontation of Strafford:

> This is no meeting, Wentworth! Tears increase
> Too hot. A thin mist—is it blood?—enwraps
> The face I loved once. (V, ii)[17]

He walks with God, and listens to the voice of England, which speaks to him and commands him:

> England,—I am thine own! Dost thou exact
> That service? I obey thee to the end.[18]

His is the final complete triumph. Strafford's moment of humiliation in III, ii, when the aging and betrayed Earl must kneel before Pym at the bar, "standing apart," prefigures that extraordinary scene in which Pym, a minister of the Lord, humiliates Charles by warning him that even kings stand in need of human aid:

> I thought, sir, could I find myself with you,
> After this trial, alone, as man to man—
> I might say something, warn you, pray you, save—
> Mark me, King Charles, save—you!
> But God must do it. Yet I warn you, sir—

(With Strafford's faded eyes yet full on me)
As you would have no deeper question moved
—"How long the Many must endure the One,"
Assure me, sir, if England give assent
To Strafford's death, you will not interfere!
Or— (IV, iii)[19]

Against such a threat Charles, never famous during his reign for the necessary wisdom that at least might have delayed his downfall, can only accede:

God forsakes me. I am in a net
And cannot move. Let all be as you say![20]

Yet only moments before, in pleading with Pym for a more merciful treatment of Strafford, Charles had enumerated all the reasons that should have
made such a surrender unthinkable: Strafford's friendship for him, his
knowledge that he had wronged his minister, his awareness that some in the
kingdom believe Strafford saved him, Strafford's pride, and even Strafford's
"wife and children, household cares . . . ." Before Pym's glaring eye (a
moment of theatre that a fine actor will exploit) Charles's courage, such as
it is, evaporates.

Browning's characterization of Pym is enriched by that very element
Firth found so distracting: Pym's belief that Strafford had committed an
act of apostasy. Pym confesses early to Vane that he can never quite forget
his friend (I, i);[21] accuses Wentworth of selling his soul for a title, and in
a moment of deep emotion calls him "ancient brother of my soul" (I, ii);[22]
and hopes for the best when Charles dissolves the Parliament:

Strafford is ours. The King detects the change,
Casts Strafford off forever, and resumes
His ancient path: no Parliament for us,
No Strafford for the King!   (II, i)[23]

He proves mistaken, and his personal shock is well communicated by a
speech made during his next encounter with the man he believes a Judas:

Do I affect
To see no dismal sign above your head
When God suspends his ruinous thunder there?
Strafford is doomed. Touch him no one of you!   (II, ii)[24]

From this moment he determines to destroy his former friend, his political
ally, the man he loved above all others. No niceties of conscience about the
Bill of Attainder, no objections raised by Rudyard, Fiennes, or Vane, can
move his hardened heart. When Fiennes says, "I never thought it could have

come to this," Pym's answer is a solemn charge of duty to an inner light:

> But I have made myself familiar, Fiennes,
> With this one thought—have walked, and sat, and slept,
> This thought before me. I have done such things,
> Being the chosen man that should destroy
> The traitor.   (IV, ii)[25]

At the very moment that Stafford, embittered by the fullness of his knowledge of the King's weakness of character, opens the door that leads to the river and the escape that Lady Carlisle has planned for him, Pym's entrance signifies the futility of Strafford's hope for a successful flight to France. It is a speech of superb rightness that Pym makes: it is the speech that Pym, in terms of the man he has revealed himself to be, *must* make at play's end:

> Have I done well? Speak, England! Whose sole sake
> I still have labored for, with disregard
> To my own heart,—for whom my youth was made
> Barren, my manhood waste, to offer up
> Her sacrifice—this friend, this Wentworth here—
> Who walked in youth with me, loved me, it may be,
> And whom, for his forsaking England's cause,
> I hunted by all means (trusting that she
> Would sanctify all means) even to the block
> Which waits for him . . . .
>
>   I do leave him now.
> I render up my charge (be witness, God!)
> To England who imposed it . . . .
> I never loved but one man—David not
> More Jonathan! Even thus, I love him now:
> And look for my chief portion in that world
> Where great hearts led astray are turned again . . . . (V, ii)[26]

The complicated reasons that make any statesman's action controversial, impossible to treat definitively, are masterfully handled in this speech: the self-dramatizing and the self-pity, the invocation of a nation's need as greater than personal ties, the hopelessly commingled cant and sincerity of the successful demagogue, are all here. Pym becomes in several ways the most dynamic, fully explored human being of Browning's play; he is everywhere credible, and on occasion even awe-inspiring.

The second major difficulty confronting Browning as he reviewed the historical documentation was this: *Stafford needed to talk to someone who could sympathize with his secret thoughts.* The record provided no convenient confidant. Away in Ireland for so many years, Wentworth had lost contact with those who had been his former allies. Charles, on whose good offices Strafford's fate depended, was not the logical choice; if Strafford had had free access to the King during his final year, the trial would never have developed as it did. Browning was clearly puzzled by the dearth of information about Strafford's relationship to his third wife, Elizabeth, daughter of Sir Godfrey Rhodes, and preferred not to speculate about it to the extent that Forster's memoir had done. But it was essential that Strafford, beset on all sides by enemies eager to see him down, should devise counter-strategy lest his case become merely pathetic (Browning, after all, subtitled his play "A Tragedy"). The choice of Lady Carlisle, a great woman of the court, friend of both the King and Queen, a wit and beauty who appealed to the imaginations of contemporary poets, was understandable. To her Strafford could pour out his resentment against Charles's shabby treatment of him; from her he could learn of the sitting of the Council and its deliberations on Scotland; with her he could rejoice at the prospect of complete triumph as soon as he revealed the conspiracy of Bedford, Essex, Brooke, Warwick, Savile, Saye, Mandeville, and Pym to bring a Scots army into England. It does not matter that most of what he says is foredoomed, unrealistic rhetoric in a whirlwind: we as spectators must know what is in his mind, and Lady Carlisle, as confidante, affords us that opportunity.

But even more: Browning suggests, with an astonishing delicacy of treatment, that Lady Carlisle loved Strafford, and forebore to reveal it because of her respect, however grudging, for his greater love for the King. She could not lure him

> from a love like that!
> Oh, let him love the King and die! 'Tis past.
> I shall not serve him worse for that one brief
> And passionate hope, silent forever now! (II, ii)[27]

Her role remains essentially passive throughout most of the play—she does not even inform him of the fact that he has been impeached—for what she exhorts Strafford to do, his character and the tides of history forbid him to accomplish. When, finally, she sets in motion the plan for his escape, she insists that credit be given Charles.

> Prove the King faithless, and I take away
> All Strafford cares to live for: let it be—
> 'Tis the King's scheme! (IV, i)[28]

This failure of Strafford to recognize either the depth or the quality of Lady

Carlisle's devotion is consistently developed. His wondering question, "You love me, child?" (V, ii),[29] is simply a final inquiry about the love of a follower. That Browning refused to believe that Lady Carlisle was Strafford's mistress—Forster's memoir is more speculative on this whole matter of Strafford's private life—testifies to a considered judgment on the poet's part. Indeed, the restraint of Lady Carlisle in disclosing her unworthy love for a man who has consecrated himself to another cause is one of Browning's finer touches of characterization.

The third problem was that *Charles, a man who unerringly did the wrong thing, had to be presented as a king worthy of Strafford's love.* On this score Browning's success was more limited. The historical facts show a King determined to throw away his crown, and—alienated by Charles the reckless monarch—Browning's sympathies were not enlisted by Charles the human being. Vane's accusation,

... it may be fear or craft,
As bids him pause at each fresh outrage (I, i),[30]

is unperceptive; a third explanation, stupidity, suggests itself more readily on the basis of Charles's vacillations within the play. When the King confers an earldom on Strafford, he declares that "henceforth touching Strafford is/To touch the apple of my sight"; but minutes later he can scarcely tell the Queen that the calling of the Irish Parliament was Strafford's idea rather than his own, and he regards as enlightened statecraft his decision to "buy the leaders off" (I, ii).[31] Swayed by Vane's reasoning, without consulting Strafford, he rejects the six subsidies that the English Parliament has offered, demanding twelve subsidies or nothing, and when Strafford points out to him the enormity of the mistake he has committed, shifts the blame to "old Vane's ill-judged vehemence."[32] He slanders Strafford by accusing him of having advised the war, which is now going badly;[33] and when Pym, Hampden, and Vane enter for an explanation of why he has dissolved the Parliament, willingly allows Strafford to shoulder the responsibility for having advised the action.[34] His inordinate delay in defending the man whom Hollis rightly calls "the sole roof-tree/Which props this quaking House of Privilege"[35] is appalling testimony to his executive abilities, as are his incoherent, emotional schemes to incite Percy to fall on the Parliament with an army, thereby freeing Strafford and (presumably) ending popular discontent.[36] His crumbling before Pym's demand that he sign the Bill of Attainder is of a piece with the childish disguise by which he enters the Tower of London to gaze upon his handiwork, a discredited and dying Strafford. And Browning, in giving to Charles a final speech of foredoomed bravura, may have been thinking of Shakespeare's Richard II:

> The Parliament!—go to them: I grant all
> Demands. Their sittings shall be permanent:
> Tell them to keep their money if they will:
> I'll come to them for every coat I wear
> And every crust I eat: only I choose
> To pardon Strafford. As the Queen shall choose!
> —You never heard the People howl for blood,
> Beside!   (V, ii)[37]

But to understand why Strafford should love such a man, one must recognize the full dimensions of Browning's dilemma; for the fourth problem faced by the poet, working with the life he and Forster had written, was simply this: *Strafford, acting as minister to a King who continually betrayed him, could have been under no illusions about Charles's character; his decision to remain loyal insured his death; reasons had to be found to make such a decision convincing.* These reasons were not in the public or private records of the seventeenth century, and Browning had to reconstruct imaginatively the process of reasoning whereby a glintingly sardonic intelligence could subscribe itself wholly to Charles's cause.

One matter of some concern to this play is Strafford's health. Although only forty-six when he returned to England, Thomas Wentworth was known to be a very sick man. Pym, announcing his arrival, strikes the note:

> Wentworth's come: nor sickness, care,
> The ravaged body nor the ruined soul,
> More than the winds and waves that beat his ship,
> Could keep him from the King.   (I, i)[38]

Wentworth knows the truth about the condition of his health. Speaking to Lady Carlisle, he resolves to remain calm.

> How else shall I do all I come to do,
> Broken, as you may see, body and mind,
> How shall I serve the King? Time wastes meanwhile. . . .
>   (I, ii)[39]

Even Charles, alarmed by Strafford's appearance, urges his minister to spare himself: "You are so sick, they tell me." (I, ii)[40] The Queen sneers, after his departure, "Why, he looks yellower than ever!" *(Ibid.)*[41] One of the more touching, and quietly beautiful, moments of the play materializes when Strafford, about to leave for the Scottish War, speaks to Lady Carlisle thus:

> I shall make a sorry soldier, Lucy!
> All knights begin their enterprise, we read,
> Under the best of auspices; 'tis morn,
> The Lady girds his sword upon the Youth
> (He's always very young)—the trumpets sound,
> Cups pledge him, and, why, the King blesses him—
> You need not turn a page of the romance
> To learn the Dreadful Giant's fate. Indeed,
> We've the fair Lady here; but she apart,—
> A poor man, rarely having handled lance,
> And rather old, weary, and far from sure
> His Squires are not the Giant's friends. (II, ii)[42]

Another such moment comes in V, ii, when Strafford, sitting with his children, sings to them an Italian boat-song; the autumnal mood leads to reminiscences of Venice, which Strafford visited when he was young, and to reflections on the caprices of Fame and Time.

There is, in brief, a sense of irrevocable commitment about Strafford's behavior. He has used up his energies; little enough is left for what Charles needs; and when Charles, stung by a reproof, asks whether Strafford is being disrespectful, his minister's answer is illuminating:

> My liege, do not believe it! I am yours,
> Yours ever: 'tis too late to think about:
> To the death, yours. (II, ii)[43]

This belief that wasting time, or the frailties of flesh, may interfere with duty, is very strong in Strafford. Neither Lady Carlisle nor John Pym can understand it fully; hence their efforts to make Strafford change his course; hence his rebuffs of what, after all, is kindly meant. He never seriously considers the possibility of deviating from his course. *It is too late to think about.* He is convinced that only he can save Charles:

> I have no right to hide the truth. 'Tis I
> Can save you: only I. (I, ii)[44]

The knowledge of impending death from natural causes underscores his urgency.

The fact that Charles is unworthy of such allegiance does not escape Strafford, and indeed the play resounds with Strafford's denunciations of the King's caprices. "You know him," he says sadly to Lady Carlisle at one point, "there's no counting on the King." (III, ii)[45] At another moment, impassioned with fury, he tears off the Order of the Garter and cries, "I tread a gewgaw underfoot,/And cast a memory from me." (III, iii)[46] But at the last he finds it in himself to forgive, even to ask forgiveness from, the King:

> I had forgotten
> Your education, trials, much temptation,
> Some weakness: there escaped a peevish word—
> 'Tis gone: I bless you at the last.   (V, ii)[47]

He will not flee for his own sake, for that of Lady Carlisle or of his children; but for the King, for that "awful head," yes, he will open the door, knowing that before him lies "something ominous and dark,/Fatal, inevitable."[48] He is the King's to the death.

Perhaps Browning's explanation, which amounts to the hypothesis that Strafford's illness made any other course of action impossible, and at least kept consistent and whole a foolish faith, is not wholly convincing; but it does not contradict known facts, and, like the answers that Browning worked out to his other problems in dramatizing Strafford's fate, it may be the best that any dramatist can come up with. Browning's use of his historical sources, taken all in all, is enlightened and at times brilliant. It is certainly better than Firth gave it credit for being.

The failings of *Strafford* as a play are manifest enough: the assumption that a nineteenth-century audience is deeply conversant with the events of a troubled, complex period some two centuries earlier; the irritating mannerism whereby one speaker finishes the sentence of an earlier speaker, and in turn has his sentence finished for him by a third speaker; the compact imagery which must frequently militate against effective elocution and stage business; the confusingly compressed passage of time; and the nagging suspicion of Strafford's unheroic stature that most readers will have. But that Browning's interpretation of Strafford's life traduces history is not an additional failing to be marked against the play. A sympathetic reading can hardly fail to confirm Browning's own judgment, contained in his preface to the first edition: "The portraits are, I think, faithful . . . ."[49]

NOTES

1. An invitation proffered at a dinner on May 26, 1836. W. Hall Griffin and H. C. Minchin, *The Life of Robert Browning*, 3rd ed. (London, 1938), p. 107.

2. Joseph W. Reed, "Browning and Macready: The Final Quarrel," *PMLA*, LXXV (Dec., 1960), 597-603.

3. *Pippa Passes*, first of the *Bells and Pomegranates* series, is more of a poem than a play, and, at any rate, is an exception to this generalization.

4. *A Browning Handbook*, 2nd ed. (New York [1955]), 63.

5. *Robert Browning's Prose Life of Strafford*, Browning Soc. (London, 1892), p. xiii.

6. *Ibid.*, pp. xxiv-xxv.

7. *Ibid.*, p. lxviii.

8. *The Complete Poetical Works of Robert Browning*, ed. Horace E. Scudder (Cambridge, Mass., 1895), p. 68. Hereafter cited as *Works*.

9. *Ibid.*

10. *Ibid.*, p. 72.

11. *Ibid.*, p. 67.

12. *Robert Browning's Prose Life*, p. lxvi.

13. *Ibid.*, p. viii.

14. *Works*, p. 50.

15. H. B. Charlton, "Browning as Dramatist," *Bulletin of the John Rylands Library*, XXIII (1939), 33-67.

16. *Works*, p. 51.

17. *Ibid.*, p. 74.

18. *Ibid.*

19. *Ibid.*, p. 69.

20. *Ibid.*

21. *Ibid.*, p. 52.

22. *Ibid.*, p. 54.

23. *Ibid.*, p. 57.

24. *Ibid.*, p. 59.

25. *Ibid.*, p. 68.

26. *Ibid.*, p. 73.

27. *Ibid.*, p. 59.

28. *Ibid.*, p. 66.

29. *Ibid.*, p. 73.

30. *Ibid.*, p. 50.

31. *Ibid.*, p. 55.

32. *Ibid.*, p. 58.

33. *Ibid.*

34. *Ibid.*

35. *Ibid.*, p. 65.

36. *Ibid.*, p. 66.

37. *Ibid.*, p. 72.

38. *Ibid.*, p. 51.

39. *Ibid.*, p. 53.

40. *Ibid.*, p. 55.

41. *Ibid.*

42. *Ibid.*, p. 59.

43. *Ibid.*, p. 57.

44. *Ibid.*, p. 55.

45. *Ibid.*, p. 62.

46. *Ibid.*, p. 65.

47. *Ibid.*, p. 72.

48. *Ibid.*, p. 73.

49. *Ibid.*, p. 49.

Liberalism and the Political Philosophy
of Thomas Hill Green

by Walter E. Sandelius

The importance of Thomas Hill Green (1836-1882), the principal philosopher of English liberalism during the late nineteenth century, has not been adequately estimated.[1] Of course Green's influence upon subsequent political thinkers, both within Great Britain and beyond, has not escaped notice. It is well enough known that the democratic version of philosophic idealism has been largely indebted to the career, outwardly unexciting though it was, of this Oxford don. Yet current materialist ideologies have somewhat obscured his significance.

No word employed in political debate has been the subject of more confused controversy than *liberalism*. In recent time, from both right and left this flag, as representing one point of view or another, has been either discounted or violently attacked. Liberalism of the Utilitarian phase, it may appear from what follows, has in part deserved the criticism from the right, however unthinking and ill-informed much of this has been. On the other side, one like Harold Laski, influential socialist of the parliamentary kind that he was, regarded liberalism as a dead doctrine. How far did he take account of T. H. Green?

I. Liberalism in General and the English Revised Version

Liberalism, it has been said, is a temper of mind rather than a doctrine. Yet a temper of mind may also have its rationale. Some clarity about fundamentals is important in time of crisis. Liberalism is a faith in reason and the uses of reason, a faith colored, as Morris Cohen said, "with a deep humility before the vision of a world so much larger than our human hopes and thoughts. If there are those who have no use for the word 'faith' they may fairly define liberalism as a rationalism that is rational enough to envisage the limitations of mere reasoning." Liberalism is a freeing, not only of mind, but of man's being. It was identified in the nineteenth century with the after-effects of the French Revolution, with representative government, the English Reform Bill, the growth of suffrage, civil liberties, the expansion of economic opportunity through the repeal of privilege; but it may be traced back to earlier elements of the Western heritage. Personal dignity and "the fair chance" were common objectives of the repeal of laws at the beginning, and of the passage of laws at the end, of the nineteenth century. Adam Smith and Jeremy Bentham had sought repeal of laws; the later revisionist liberalism advocated repeal of privilege through a measured extension of the state. Some sort of social law it is that the status quo (whatever for the time it is, whether a maximizing or a minimizing of the state) brings *cumulative* advantage to those who have the priorities. The persisting need for a continuing correction of the inequities that afford undue advantage to the successful and the strong, priorities that enable mediocrity at length to become ensconced in privilege, involves the state. Revisionist liberalism demanded more responsibility from the state, lest the enlarging collectivist orders in the so-called private sector take undue advantage of the public. Liberalism in modern times has made common cause at first with the middle class, increasingly with democracy and the common man.

Throughout Locke's philosophy of natural right, the anti-natural-law utilitarianism of Bentham and the Mills, and the religious idealism of Green persists the idea of individual right. These doctrines employ reason. While questioning all absolutes they do not do so to the end of concluding simply that no abiding truths or values exist.

Green differed, however, from both Locke and the Benthamites in their basic premises. Green revived thinking about natural law in the context of a new dynamic. Bentham had supposed this doctrine to have been demolished by Hume; but finding that job not well enough done he directed his own sledge-hammer blows against it. Yet the utilitarians too were agreed that, however valuable their aim of liberating man to use reason freely and of subjecting to its scrutiny all established orders, rules, and authorities, it is not enough to say that liberalism is a faith only in method and procedure. One cannot believe in freedom of inquiry except on the prior assumption of the right to life itself. Nor is mere life worth having if it be not a tolerable life. The right to life, and to the good life, is not merely procedural but *substantive* right.

The idea that not mere life but the *good life* is the summary end of the state goes back to the ancient Greeks. So do many of the ideas of modern liberalism. Oriental monarchies had ruled largely through fear, and had imposed conformity; but Greek merchant adventurers before the sixth century B. C., Greek scientists and philosophers from Thales to Aristotle, left after them their legacies of the free life, despite their institution of slavery and class structures. This inheritance persists. The freedom of inquiry, the attendant growth of toleration, the habit of initiative, the conception of individual right and the regard for human personality, the enforcement of a rule of law by the community itself, the anticipated creativity—these are constituents of the liberal way.

The deeper elements of this civil tradition, "the public philosophy" as it is called by Walter Lippmann, may not be clearly seen. Its intellectual foundations, though not the humanitarian element by and large, *were* largely lost to view in the Utilitarian School. That English liberalism was brought back into the main stream of Western political thought was in large part the work of T. H. Green.[2] Green, of course, did not return to the natural-law concepts of Locke—though he, too, has his share of responsibility for the recent revival of Locke, as part of the opposition to modern excesses of relativism. He criticized the fixities in Locke's conception of rights. In a modern form he represents the tradition of the higher law, with its continuity of centuries. But more to the immediate point, he was to become, more than did the J. S. Mill of the later phase, more than Herbert Spencer with his liberalist application of biological concepts, and more than the other philosophers of English idealism,[3] the creative influence of the revised liberalism that today contends on the one hand against reaction, and on the other against the materialist ideology of Marx.

II. FREEDOM, RIGHTS, AND MORALS

Green's England is that of the 1870's onward. The Liberal Party, which had drawn its original inspiration from the Benthamite Radicals and their advocacy of a minimum of state regulation, already was supporting such measures as factory regulation, grants to education, sanitary laws, land-tenure reform, and other extensions of the public power. Its dissatisfaction with the condition of the country and with the erstwhile policy of the negative state was much like the dissatisfaction of its leading exponent, J. S. Mill himself. Mill's thought in its later evolution was not systematically set forth. It fell to Green to supply a rationale for the changes in liberalism as both a movement and as a philosophy. This he was prepared to do by virtue of his natural sympathies with the middle class and with the poor, his place in the academic halls where so much of English political leadership has found its source and inspiration, his scholarly and tenacious mind, and his intense, lifelong pursuit of highest truth joined to a liking for practical politics in those various minor capacities which he found open to him. Not a few of the nation's leaders, who continued to come by way of Oxford as of old, were to be indebted to him. His influence upon subsequent English philosophy and political thought, while not so conspicuous as that of others of less originality or depth, has persisted.

The state was a negative good to the Benthamites. It has been alleged at times that it was so also to Green and his followers. The reforms urged by Green in the practical sphere contradict this view. As much as any major, non-Marxist thinker in the English-speaking world, he stood for limitations upon the traditional freedom of contract, and did so in the interests of a larger freedom, factory regulation, temperance control, restricting abuses by landowners, and promotion of the health and education of the individual generally: "To an Athenian slave, who might be used to gratify a master's lust, it would have been a mockery to speak of the state as the realization of freedom: and perhaps it would not be much less so to speak of it as such to an untaught and underfed denizen of a London yard, with gin shops on the right and on the left."[4] Or again: "Our modern legislation, then, with reference to labour, and education and health, involving, as it does, manifold interference with freedom of contract, is justified on the ground that it is the business of the State, not indeed directly to promote moral goodness, for that, from the very nature of moral goodness, it cannot do, but to maintain the conditions without which a free exercise of human faculties is impossible."[5]

This, says Lane Lancaster, "sounds like an argument in philosophic language for what Franklin Roosevelt called 'the abundant life,' and indeed it is." It is of importance that Green defended the institution of private property, while elucidating limitations prescribed by the general welfare, and while believing also that the end of a free society is not "the accumulation of comforts."

Utilitarian liberalism had developed a materialist philosophy to support a minimal state. The idealistic liberalism of the last quarter of the nineteenth century was, on the other hand, founded on the idea of a higher law which would enlist the service of the state to support a positive freedom, a freedom of self-realization through the good life. Green was religiously oriented. To him the state was a means to the end of moral goodness, a means whereby merely formal and real freedom, between liberty and law, between the interest of the individual and the common good, could be reconciled. Moral goodness as the end of the state is of the essence of that which distinguishes man from the natural order—not merely reason but a kind of self-consciousness, which, as seen by Green, has affinities with the Hegelian Absolute Mind.

According to Green's metaphysic, man's self-consciousness is part of the universal self-consciousness; human limitations in what he understands and wills, exist, but he participates in the whole. Being human, he possesses reason and will; he is self-conscious man. To be conscious is to have an object for the reason and will. Among the objects of which man is conscious is himself. Apart from the object of his self-consciousness he has no existence as what he is. A self-consciousness must include both the subjective and the objective. Consciousness can in no wise be severed from its object. The conscious in man reaches out in some sense to the whole of the interrelated universe. The objective and the subjective are not severable; the objective is universal; it follows that man's self-consciousness, too, must be part of a universal self-consciousness.

The object of the will can only be that which is thought good for the self. Green did not mean simply one's own pleasure. To have any awareness of the good of self is to be aware of the comparable good of others. Thus the universal self-consciousness can only be a concern with its own good. The true good of any partial self exists imbedded in the good of the whole.

The good of the self may be envisioned in terms of freedom. No freedom can be without a responsible opportunity for choice. Moral being, consisting of the exercise of reason and will, can realize itself only through the making of choices such as promote the good. Green held with Kant that the one supreme good is the universal good will. Freedom for the idealist consists of life in accord with the moral law. This never can be rid of the necessity and the responsibility for choice between the better and the worse; there exists a standard of the good. Moral (as distinguished from ideal) right consists of the free choosing of what one ought to choose: the common good, the individual good, the universal good, ultimately as One.

The opportunities of moral growth, however, depend also upon external circumstance. The liberty which is the direct concern of the state is that sum of inter-personal and inter-group relationships conducive to moral being. The state exists to remove the hindrances thereto. This is not to suggest a minimum of state action. But the state may not try to enter—it cannot enter —the moral sphere as such. It can at most "remove hindrances" to the exercise of that responsible volition which makes a man what he is. Of the essence of such "removal of hindrances" is the safeguarding and the promoting of the equal opportunity to each, in accord with capacity and need.

Men cannot be made good by act of parliament. The spring of morality, moreover, is the spring of man's spiritual nature. Yet this inner voice may manifest itself more or less strongly, depending upon limitations of the social milieu: the family, the state, and other group forms. Rights are conditions of the social interrelationship such as *conduce* to the moral good. At the same time, the ideal condition, while always greater than the mores, is a potential implicit *in* the mores. Rights are not primordial as in the Lockean view, but teleological in the Aristotelian sense. Are they, then, eternal forms laid in heaven? Green argues that what may be called a natural right has a changing content, and at the same time an enduring consistency. Are there not change and consistency, both, in all that lives?

Freedom, while it is contingency, is also law. This is true of both political and moral freedom. *Moral* freedom, as already said, is premised on the opportunity of the individual to err, though he does not truly achieve freedom except insofar as he does *not* sin, that is, except insofar as he has the understanding and the will to be his best self. *Political* liberty is the opportunity extended by the social condition, and in turn enforced by the state, in proportion to which the moral life may grow. *Rights*—though with the individual human being as the fundamental subject and object alike—are not thinkable except in a social context. Rights imply forbearance or obligation. *Ideal* right connotes that social condition that by its nature *can* be embodied in the mores. Thus, political liberty is opportunity subject to a social responsibility: the best conceivable responsibility for each and all. The ideal is seen, ofttimes, more clearly by a lone protesting prophet than by the contentious many of a confused generation.

Rights, however, are necessarily subject to social recognition. This point of Green's has been a stumbling block to some. If they are not rights until socially recognized, it may be said, what are they but the mores? In what sense are they to be conceived as ideal rights? Green really means that ideally they are *capable* of social recognition and of social enforcement, though he does not always state this point clearly.

Green himself, commonly uses interchangeably the words "moral" and "spiritual." What, then, is the relation of the "moral" or the "spiritual" to the "natural"?

The opposition to "naturalistic" ethics, which he adumbrates in his *Prolegomena to Ethics*, does not abandon his often-expressed view that nature is the first stage of God's revelation of himself. The pursuit of truth, he holds, is "in principle identical with the striving after God which animates the moral life." By "spiritual" he meant "the natural rightly understood," and by moral life "not an escape from, but a completion of, physical processes." As the editor of his *Works* and one of his best interpreters, A. L. Nettleship, has written:

In his own mind there could be no competition between laws of nature and laws of morality, for he regarded the former as stages in the self-development of the same mind as the latter; but when men of science first treat the facts which they have established as final and independent existences, and then proceed to include among them the principle of which they are the partial expression and without which they would not be facts at all, they seemed to him to be misunderstanding their own procedure, and to be on a track which must lead to the stultification not only of moral aspiration but of the scientific impulse itself. He would have adopted the saying that science tells us what is, not what ought to be, not in the sense that the actual and the ideal are two independent worlds, but in the sense that any particular branch of experience, while it may be, and for practical purposes must be, treated as self-contained, is in truth related at every point to something which goes beyond it . . . and which necessitates the conversion of the mere 'is' into an 'ought to be' ("Memoir" in *Works,* III, cxliii-cxliv).

This thought is stated by Green as follows:

If it is true on the one hand that the interpretation of nature by the supposition of ends external to it, with reference to which its processes are directed, has been discarded, and that its rejection has been the condition of growth in an exact knowledge of nature, on the other hand the recognition of ends immanent in nature, of ideas realized within it, is the basis of a scientific explanation of life. The phenomena of life are not ideal, in the sense in which the ideal is opposed to that which is sensibly verifiable, but they are related to the processes of material change which are their conditions, as ideas or ideal ends which those processes contribute to realize, because, while they determine the processes (while the processes would not be what they are but for relation to them), yet they are *not* those processes, *not* identical with any one or number of them, or all of them together (II, 437).

Idealism, as he says elsewhere, is "not the admission of an ideal world of guess and aspiration alongside of the empirical, but the recognition of the empirical itself as ideal" (I, 179), which "trusts, not to a guess as to what is beyond experience, but to analysis of what is within it" (I, 449).

The 'is' of the moment is a mingling, in some proportion, of the ideal with its imperfection. Perfection will never be wholly and humanly grasped. However, a consciousness that ideal aims are actualities at work in every living experience, an awareness that the 'is' of the moment is the potential of the more of that which it already is, the knowledge that the 'ought to be' is but one face of the *larger* 'is,' strengthens the good—the good of each and of all.

The debate between Green and the utilitarians (Henry Sidgwick, for example) on the relation of pleasure to the good, is beyond the limits of this paper. The hedonistic creed had been roundly attacked by Ruskin, Carlyle, and others to whom Green acknowledged his debt; but, unlike Carlyle, Green held democratic sympathies. In the matter of proposed social reforms, he had less in common with these men, again especially with Carlyle, than with the utilitarians whose contributions to the national well-being he freely acknowledged. The widespread influence which the doctrines of the latter had achieved he attributed to the character and conspicuous ability of the leaders of this school, which "had the great lesson to teach, that the value of all laws and institutions, the rectitude of all conduct, was to be estimated by reference to the well-being of all men, and that in the estimate of that well-being no nation or class or individual was to count above another." The acceptance of this lesson in practice, "not the theory that the end of life is pleasure," had made utilitarianism a power for good.

There is a degree of philosophical utilitarianism in Green, too, though it has been largely put aside in favor of the Kantian and Hegelian influence. He largely shared the practical objectives of the contemporary utilitarians. He worked hard for the improvement of middle-class education. All English youth—he believed—should have the chance to become gentlemen at institutions that would alter the methods by which the so-called public schools now develop the "conventional character of the English gentleman." He struggled for temperance laws, and for protection of the poor against privilege embedded in the law. He opposed foreign policies that would increase the risk of involvement in war. During America's Civil War he strongly espoused the Northern cause, writing to his sister: "I should be sorry to have you believe the nonsense which the *Times* writes about the most important struggle that the world has seen since the French Revolution." War against the North "would make England a wretched country to live in for the term of our lives at least." He attacked the shallowness of educated English opinion on the subject. As for philosophic foundations, "The fabric of European society stands apparently square and strong on a basis of decent actual equity, but no rationale of this equity is generally recognized. The hedonism of Hume has been turned into utilitarianism, the jacobinism of Rousseau into a gentle liberalism, but neither *ism* could save the 'culture' of England, in the great struggle between willfulness and social right across the Atlantic, from taking sides with the willfulness. Whatever might be the case practically, it had not learnt speculatively that freedom means something else than doing what one likes. A philosophy based on feeling was still playing the anarch in its thoughts" (III, 117).

Freedom is no mere absence of restraint. This was the Hegelian lesson that needed to be learned. How far is Green justly charged with an Hegelianism that is not followed out to its necessary conclusions? Since he accepted the premise of the general will, should this logically have taken him away from his democratic predilections?

III. GREEN VERSUS HEGEL; THE POLITICAL AND THE SPIRITUAL

Green stood closer to Kant than to Hegel, and was greatly concerned about clarifying the obscurities and correcting the inconsistencies of Kant. "The vital truth" which he found in Hegel was: "That there is one spiritual self-conscious being, of which all that is real is the activity or expression; that we are related to this being, not merely as parts of the world which is its expression, but as partakers in some inchoate measure of the self-consciousness through which it at once constitutes and distinguishes itself from the world, and that this participation is the source of morality and religion" (III, 146). But the conception that "the objective world, in its actual totality, is thought," rather than the materiality that manifests the idea, requires us to remember also that the processes of human intelligence "are but reflections of that real thought under the conditions of a limited nature." This recognition of the imperfect and the limited in all of man's thinking and action is what Hegel himself did not well remember, though he too had said the same. Hegel makes "leaps in the dark," as when, unaccountably (for a philosopher), he identifies the march of God on earth with the Prussian monarchy. Both he and Rousseau posit an ideal reality, called by Rousseau the general will, and by Hegel, more often, the Deity. The "real" will of man, according to Rousseau, is for his own true good an extension beyond his conscious desire in the particular. All men in some measure share an intimation of the good beyond conscious thought and desire. Similarly, Hegel regards the true good as beyond conscious realization and intent. Yet in justifying the ways of God to man, Hegel in general sees the good transpiring even where the strong appearance is that of an injustice and wrong. This tendency to justify whatever is, is carried to an absurd extreme. It confuses the proposition that in the long run right is might with the proposition that the particular of the moment is to be seen as itself the right.

So also Rousseau, identifying the general will with right, and being concerned with the implications of this idea in the political realm, initially distinguishes between the general will and what he calls the "will of all." The distinction becomes obscure. One finds him talking about the general will when he can only be referring to an actual consensus, or, alternatively, to a majority, in either case to a *practical* representative rather than to the full ideal of the sovereign will. Green, at times, will speak loosely of "right" as something conditioned by social recognition, as if by this he means recognition in the actual mores, when he can only have in mind, as he has made clear elsewhere, an ideal social right. At least a partial apology may be made for Green in this regard: his life span was only forty-six years, and most of his work was posthumously edited and published.

It is not necessary to adopt wholly, or largely, the doctrine of the general will in order to perceive the truth that is in it. One may think with Kant that man has a direct sense of obligation, rather than see duty as the reflection of the self's pursuit of its own satisfaction. Yet if the particularized self is seen as emanation of a universal self-concern identical with a universal other-concern, the Kantian and the Hegelian premises are not far apart in their relating the reason to the will and the will to the reason. This may be said without prejudice to Kant's insistence upon the ultimate as unknowable. So, too, Rousseau's general will is a concept of reason no less than of will.

Rousseau's confusion at times of the ideal with the actual has obscured his meaning. In his discussion of the practical business of how right shall become manifest in the community, he argues that only in the very small community is the functioning of the general will possible. Certain modern critics have held that, whatever value the concept of the general will may have had for the small community of primitive times, or of Rousseau's imagination, it can have no meaning for the enlarged community of a later day. Yet if the ideal is really perceived, then its meaning for the larger stage will be seen as well. Man's ideal is always short of realization, while at the same time a veritable reality. The ideal is always at work in the reality, and the reality of the state is to be seen not less in man's aspiration than in crystallized history. The past is not more alive, more real, than is the future. The future is very much the substance of man's hope, man's hope very much his present reality.

Green, in his day, did not think largely in terms of the state as an evolution beyond the nation-state. But he had much to say about right in relation to peace and war, and his idealism, applied to a democratic purpose, was more far-seeing than the authoritarianism of Hegel. Though he thought Hegel in many ways to have been *the* philosopher of modern times, he was distrustful of Hegelian "leaps in the dark." He did not, like Hegel, identify freedom largely with the *objectified* state and with the status quo. He preferred to start with Kantian propositions and move toward his own conclusions. With thoroughness (and at times at a pedestrian pace) he would unravel the tangles—not invariably with clear statements of his own. Though he held that feeling, on the whole, achieves a surer insight than does the reason, his logic was more rigorous than that of Hegel, possibly not less so

48

than that of Kant himself, and in some particulars more. He had, of course, added to his mastery of Greek thought, the benefit of Kant's great work.

The issue is whether Green has a reasonably consistent view of the relation of the individual to the state; whether the individual appears clearly pre-eminent over the state, and not, as with Hegel, the state over the individual. To Green, moreover, the state, as but means to the individual good, is to be distinguished from society. Rights, as belonging to individuals, can be understood only in their social context, and as such are prior to the state. While "will, not force, is the foundation of the state," yet the state is that organized coercive power that exists to serve the end of rights. At least logically, if not chronologically, society comes before the state, for the whole comes before the part. If rights exist at all, they pertain to the individual as member of some social group. The state in its most primitive form, no doubt, was not clearly differentiated from the familial relationship. The state exists to enforce rights that it did not originally create. It legalizes basic rights of the individual in the community and implements the same with legal prescriptions of its own creation. In this sense, according to Green, rights may be said to derive *from* the state. Ideally the state is the perfect guarantor of rights. This does not mean that there can be no right to challenge the objectified state. Yet, unless the established state is perverted to the extent that the flow of justice through its channels becomes impossible, disobedience is likely to lead only to wider chaos or to the increase of evils. The state is to be challenged only with fear and trembling, yet it is not beyond challenge. It exists but to serve the right and the good of individual man.

Is resistance to be justified always by the fact that the majority approves? Green answers that resistance may be made "not because the majority approve it, but because it is for the public good" (*Political Obligation*, p. 117). He has no clear, automatically applicable test for recognizing the situation that would justify resistance. But neither has any other theory (except that which makes the majority opinion the right opinion). Yet it does not take the genius of a Mill to perceive that a tyranny of the majority may also exist. It may be said at least that, over some period of time, the *extremities* of injustice *are* recognized by the generality of mandkind, as well as by the generality of the philosophic schools despite their differences.

Green observed that even selfish and unjust rulers like Napoleon have served, despite themselves, causes greater than themselves. But he did not justify or excuse the iniquity of rulers. On the contrary, he is at pains to show that good comes only from good motives, though the evil-minded may unwittingly have served the purposes of the good. They would have done even more if they had been impelled by right motives. The spirit of the argument here is unlike the spirit of Hegel's talk of the "world-historical" heroes, like Caesar or Napoleon, whose "conduct . . . [often] obnoxious to moral reprehension" he would defend as inevitable in the part of "so mighty a form."[6]

The metaphysical theory of the state, in its Hegelian form, has received its merited criticism, if not demolition, at the hands of L. T. Hobhouse.[7] But Hobhouse did not identify the idealism of Green with that of Hegel. It has been charged that a more logical progression in Green's thought would have led him nearer to Hegel, as it did Bosanquet; contrary to this judgment, Green was the most logical of the three. His works have had great influence upon, and have been highly praised by, distinguished thinkers, including such recent notable scholars as A. L. Nettleship, Professor E. Caird, the late Lord Birker (formerly A. D. Lindsay, Master of Balliol), Sir Ernest Barker, and others. Our purpose has been to stress, it is hoped not too tritely, the following points: Green viewed the state as the servant of the moral order; the individual as the human repository of moral being and as the end of the state; the core of the individual as a self-conscious reason and will responsible to a universal self-consciousness, to which Green gives the name of God; and the positive function of the state as maintaining the opportunity of moral and spiritual growth.

Will materialist presuppositions in sectors of Western liberalism, as well as in Marxism, conspire in a confused competition with conservatism and reaction to obscure our growing insight into moral reality? Materialist trends in Western thought have led, despite the achievements of science, to the atheism and the immoral in modern communism, the debt of Marx to Hegel notwithstanding. Abroad, in our world, however, is a spiritualizing of thought. The growing prestige of new theologies, and recent contributions by psychological science, hasten the decay of materialism. We remember the thinking of Green as one who combined extraordinary mystic insight with a severe reason applied to the political problem.

A. L. Nettleship has said:

The quality of mind which distinguished him in practical life followed him into philosophy. In both he showed the same combination of simplicity and depth, of homeliness and elevation, of limitation and comprehension. While the whole of his metaphysic might be said to be little more than a prolonged attempt to get to the bottom of the question, What is a fact of experience? an occasional remark shows that in his mind this apparently simple question involved that of the nature of the world and of God. And though he had neither the varied information which can illustrate and enforce the bare results of thought, nor the plastic impulse which divines the whole before it knows the details, yet even when he was most abstract and difficult he always gave the impression of having his feet upon the ground, and if there is little external system in his writings, there is hardly a page upon which the unity of his mind has not left its mark ("Memoir" in *Works*, III, lxxxvi).

Similarly, Professor E. Caird has written that Green was one who scarcely

felt that he had a scientific right to any principle which he had not submitted to a testing process for years, and who never satisfied himself—as men of idealistic tendencies are apt to satisfy themselves—with an intuitive grasp of any comprehensive idea, until he had vindicated every element of it by the hard toil of an exhaustive reflection. . . . In this he showed how a deep faith in certain principles may be united with the questioning temper of science, and even with a scrupulous skepticism which is ever ready to go back to the beginning, that it may exhaust everything that can be said against them. For such a mind . . . appropriate activity must be rather to lay and try the foundations than to build the superstructure. But it is the result of such work, and such work alone, to secure that the foundations are immovably fixed upon the rock.[8]

If man's experience bears out the evidence of a spiritual reality that sustains his being more surely than does the materialist premise, for example, of Marx or of Freud—the contributions that these men made to the understanding of the human nature and experience notwithstanding—then the influence of Green's idealism doubtless will continue to grow beyond the nineteenth century.

Idealism as a philosophy has been contrasted by some with the Christian point of view. This assumes a narrow premise for the latter. Was Green a Christian? What does it mean to be a Christian? To quote Nettleship, "If it means to believe that every man has God in him, that religion is a continual death of a lower and a coming to life of a higher self, and that these truths were more vividly realized in thought and life by Jesus of Nazareth and some of his followers than by any other known men, then without doubt he was a Christian. If it means that the above truths depend upon the fact that Jesus was born and died under conditions impossible to other human beings, then equally without doubt he was not a Christian" (*op. cit.*, page c). With all his extensive research in biblical sources, Green had little interest in the distinction between orthodoxy and heterodoxy, and "its attendant babel of controversy. . . ; not because he wished to shirk unpleasant questions, nor because he was not clear as to what he believed, but because he cared about the reality of religion and not about its accessories, and was convinced that its reality does not depend upon its dogmatic expression" (*ibid.*). He did not deny the possibility of extraordinary spiritual phenomena, but would give himself, rather, to that higher reality of which these are but one expression. The political questions had for him no mean significance. He would perhaps think today, with Arnold Toynbee, that for mankind to save itself after the middle of the twentieth century requires hardly less than a "transfiguration" of the human being himself. He would, at any rate, give to the issue of the state, grown vastly more critical than in his own day, the whole of his tenacious mind, and with certain belief in an overruling Benevolence.

NOTES

1. *Works of Thomas Hill Green,* ed. by R. L. Nettleship, vol. I-III (London, Longmans, 1906). Except where otherwise indicated, quotations from the writings of Green will be cited in the text of this paper only by volume and page referring to this standard edition.

2. George H. Sabine, in his masterly *History of Political Theory* (New York, 3rd ed., 1961), well summarizes the general aspect of the "revisionist liberalism" of the last quarter of the century. He gives principal credit to Green, who was "more coherently liberal in his political theory than John Stuart Mill," adding, like other commentators, that his idealism, though calling itself neo-Hegelian, contained "not a trace . . . of the political authoritarianism that Hegelianism connoted in Germany" (p. 705).

3. Here, and in all mention of idealism in what follows, the reference is to *objective* idealism, and not to *subjective* idealism of the Berkeleyan kind.

4. *Lectures on the Principles of Political Obligation,* 1948 reprint from the original publication in Volume II of *Works,* p. 8.

5. Quoted by Lane Lancaster, *Masters of Political Thought* (Boston, 1959), III *(Hegel to Dewey),* 215-216. Dr. Lancaster, eminent scholar that he is, seems to me unduly severe in his strictures upon Green, yet to make a very valuable contribution upon this "master," as he does notably upon all the others considered by him.

6. The above paragraph is occasioned by a reference to Hegel in Lancaster's stimulating and provocative chapter on Green (*ibid.,* pp. 233-234).

7. *The Metaphysical Theory of the State* (London, 1918). This vigorous attack against Hegelianism, written in reaction to World War I, while well reasoned and effective as a scholarly onslaught upon the Leviathan state, does not include a thorough consideration of Green. It has had, probably, more to do than has any other single work with diminishing Green's reputation. Hobhouse, while he had much in common with Green's humane democracy, found his analysis confusing, taking particular exception to the saying that "rights are made by recognition. There is no right but thinking makes it so" (p. 119). It is true that Green's expression here is not adequate to his concern with the *ideal.* One must read Green in his entirety, as well as with some allowance for slips of tongue and pen. Most of his lectures, while based upon fairly full manuscript, were never gone over with finality by himself before publication.

8. From the preface to *Essays in Philosophical Criticism,* ed. by Andrew Seth and R. B. Haldane (London, 1883).

BIBLIOGRAPHY

Original Sources

The Works of Thomas Hill Green, 3 volumes, ed. R. L. Nettleship (London, 1896). "Memoir" by Green's pupil, Nettleship, is included in Vol. III. *Prolegomena to Ethics,* ed. A. C. Bradley (2nd ed., Oxford, 1884). *Lectures in the Principles of Political Obligation,* originally Volume II of the Philosophical Works (1885-88), with an introduction by A. D. Lindsay (London, 1941).

Principal Commentaries and General Works

Barker, Ernest, *Political Thought in England: 1848-1914* (2nd ed., London, 1950), chs. II-III.

Brinton, Crane, *English Political Thought in the Nineteenth Century* (London, 1933).

Carritt, E. F., *Morals and Politics: Theories of Their Relation from Hobbes and Spinoza to Marx and Bosanquet* (Oxford, 1935), especially ch. X.

Chin, Y. L., *The Political Theory of Thomas Hill Green* (New York, 1920).

Fairbrother, W. H., *The Philosophy of T. H. Green* (2nd ed., London, 1900).

Harris, Frederick P., *The Neo-Idealist Political Theory: Its Continuity with the British Tradition* (New York, 1944).

Hearnshaw, F. J. C., *The Social and Political Ideas of Some Representative Thinkers of the Victorian Age* (London, 1933), ch. 7.

Hobhouse, L. T., *Liberalism* (London, 1911).

Hobhouse, L. T., *The Metaphysical Theory of the State* (London, 1918).

Lancaster, Lane W., *Masters of Political Thought* (Boston, 1959), III (*Hegel to Dewey*), ch. 6.

Laski, Harold J., *The Rise of Liberalism* (New York and London, 1936).

Lippincott, Benjamin E., *The Victorian Critics of Democracy* (Minneapolis, 1938).

MacCunn, J., *Six Radical Thinkers* (London, 1907), ch. VI.

Muirhead, J. H., *The Service of the State: Four Lectures on the Political Teaching of T. H. Green* (London, 1908).

Ritchie, D. G., *The Principles of State Interference* (London, 1891), ch. IV.

Sabine, George H., *A History of Political Theory* (3rd ed., New York, 1961), especially chs. XXXI-XXXII.

Sidgwick, Henry, *The Ethics of T. H. Green, Herbert Spencer and J. Martineau* (London, 1902), the first eight lectures relating to Green's *Prolegomena to Ethics.*

Watkins, Frederick M., *The Political Tradition of the West: A Study in the Development of Modern Liberalism* (Cambridge, Mass., 1948).

Weldon, T. D., *States and Morals: A Study in Political Conflicts* (London, 1946), ch. 3.

The Intruder-Motif in George Eliot's Fiction

By George J. Worth

The novels of George Eliot have often been described as dealing primarily with the interaction between human character and the social environment. All the critics of her work from the beginning have either pointed this out or taken it for granted, and the idea has been given special prominence in two of the excellent studies of George Eliot which have appeared in recent years, Joan Bennett's *George Eliot* and Jerome Thale's *The Novels of George Eliot*.

It has not been sufficiently stressed, however, that most of the genuinely interesting characters in her fiction are seriously at odds with their social environments, and may even be said to be intruders in the worlds they inhabit. This intrusion is of two sorts. In numerous cases it is physical intrusion: the character enters a circumscribed area from the outside, and his values and beliefs clash with the dominant values and beliefs of his new associates in such a way as to carry the plot forward and expose the theme significantly. Such intruders include Amos Barton, the Countess Czerlaski, Caterina Sarti, and Tryan in the *Scenes of Clerical Life,* Hetty Sorrel and Dinah Morris in *Adam Bede,* Silas Marner, Tito Melema in *Romola,* Harold Transome in *Felix Holt,* and Lydgate, Ladislaw, and Bulstrode in *Middlemarch.* In other instances, there is no physical intrusion, but the character's sense of alienation from the world he lives in is just as strong as if there had been: he (or, almost always, she) has lived in a given society from birth or early infancy, but again there is a fundamental conflict between individual and social values and beliefs. In this group we may number Maggie Tulliver in *The Mill on the Floss*, Romola, Esther Lyon in *Felix Holt*, Dorothea Brooke in *Middlemarch*, and Gwendolen Harleth and Daniel in *Daniel Deronda*.

I

In the closed provincial societies which George Eliot habitually depicted, the mere fact that a person was an outsider earned him the suspicion of the natives. Even Bulstrode, the wealthy banker who had lived in Middlemarch for years, "as a man not born in the town, and altogether of dimly-known origin, was considered to have done well in uniting himself with a real Middlemarch family" (ch. xi); the solid citizens, reluctant to accept him, "wished to know who his father and grandfather were, observing that five-

and-twenty years ago nobody had ever heard of a Bulstrode in Middle-march" (ch. xiii).

Nevertheless, more than this kind of vague antipathy was always involved in the distrust or dislike with which George Eliot's intruders were regarded by their neighbors. Most often, it was a question of theology. In the pre-Reform Bill world of which she wrote in all her English novels except *Daniel Deronda*, religious heterodoxy was a serious matter. The Established Church was still very powerful, but much of what passed for its strength was in truth complacency and flabbiness. Aware of this, enlightened churchmen were far more disturbed by Dissent and the Evangelical movement than they would have been under different circumstances, and their less enlightened co-religionists felt all the hostility in the presence of new ideas which is characteristic of narrow minds. Provincial ignorance played a large part in the religious intolerance with which George Eliot dealt. In the *Scenes of Clerical Life*, for example, the positive Mr. Dempster is able to persuade his barroom audience that "the word presbyterian is derived from John Presbyter, a miserable fanatic who wore a suit of leather, and went about from town to village, and from village to hamlet, inoculating the vulgar with the asinine virus of Dissent" ("Janet's Repentance," ch. i), and in the same story Evangelicalism is viewed by the townspeople of Milby as "a murrain or blight all the more terrible, because its nature was but dimly conjectured" (ch. iii).

Barton in the first of the *Scenes* and Tryan in the third (unlike their counterpart, Gilfil, in the middle story of the volume), outsiders both, are Evangelical clergymen who encounter hostility and opposition in their new parishes because they preach a more challenging version of Christianity than that to which their parishioners are accustomed. Barton's difficulties are complicated by his ungainliness and social ineptitude, but the basic source of friction is the same in both cases: each man has imported a new and uncongenial brand of religion into the community. Mrs. Patten in "The Sad Fortunes of the Rev. Amos Barton" is typical in her complaint: "'I don't understand these new sort o' doctrines. When Mr. Barton comes to see me, he talks about nothing but my sins and my need o' marcy. Now, Mr. Hackit, I've never been a sinner. From the fust beginning, when I went into service, I al'ys did my duty by my emplyers. . . . If I'm not to be saved, I know a many as are in a bad way'" (ch. i). Barton puzzles or offends so many of his flock with his innovations and his bumbling that he has virtually no fund of good will to draw on when his questionable involvement with the Countess Czerlaski begins.

Tryan's Evangelical preaching arouses alarm for a different reason: it is too effective. Although he is "the first Evangelical clergyman who had risen above the Milby horizon," he makes very considerable inroads in that parish. Before long, "Evangelicalism was no longer a nuisance existing merely in by-corners, which any well-clad person could avoid; it was invading the very drawing-rooms, mingling itself with the comfortable fumes of port-wine and brandy, threatening to deaden with its murky breath all the splendour of the ostrich feathers, and to stifle Milby ingenuousness, not pretending to be better than its neighbours, with a cloud of cant and lugubrious hypocrisy" (ch ii).

Although her doctrines are as unsettling to her hearers as Barton's and Tryan's are to theirs, Dinah Morris in *Adam Bede* occupies a different position. She is not as dependent on public opinion among those to whom she preaches as a beneficed clergyman of the Church of England would be, and she is more boldly in defiance of that opinion, as a woman, a Methodist, and a daughter of bleak Stonyshire addressing herself to the comfortable inhabitants of Loamshire. The simple folk of Hayslope do not know what to make of this phenomenon, but insofar as they understand it they are disturbed. As the uneasy parish clerk complains to his vicar,

"there's no knowin' what'll come, if we're t' have such preachins as that a-goin' on ivery week—there'll be no livin' i' th' village. For them Methodisses make folks believe as if they take a mug o' drink extry, an' make theirselves a bit comfortable, they'll have to go to hell fo't as sure as they're born. I'm not a tipplin' man nor a drunkard—nobody can say it on me—but I like a extry quart at Easter or Christmas time, as is nat'ral when we're goin' the rounds a'singin', an' folks offer't you for nothin'; or when I'm a-collectin' the dues; an' I like a pint wi' my pipe, an' a neighbourly chat at Mester Casson's now an' then, for I was brought up i' the Church, thank God, an' ha' been a parish clerk this two-an'-thirty year: I should know what the church religion is" (ch. v).

Because her role in Hayslope is so different from Barton's in Shepperton or Tryan's in Milby, Dinah's religious ideas do not split the community as deeply. Nevertheless, a wide gulf yawns between her theological views and those of Adam, who represents all that is best in the village in which he has grown up. " 'I'm not for laughing at no man's religion. Let 'em follow their consciences, that's all. Only I think it ud' be better if their consciences 'ud let 'em stay quiet i' the church—there's a deal to be learnt there. And there's such a thing as being oversperitial; we must have something besides Gospel i' this world' " (ch. i). Though this is the rather smug Adam as yet untouched by tragedy who speaks, we have no reason to believe that he changes his mind about this matter in the course of his bitter experiences. And it is precisely because George Eliot is so unconvincing on the question of how the doctrinal gulf between Adam and Dinah is bridged that so many readers are dissatisfied with the denouement of the novel.

Silas Marner's conflict with the people of Raveloe is far more central to his novel than Dinah's difficulties in Hayslope are to *Adam Bede*. Like Dinah, he is a Dissenter rather than merely an Evangelical. Like her, too, he comes to a fertile, prosperous country from a grim manufacturing town. But, unlike Dinah, he intends his move to be permanent, and he runs into the animosity of the stolid villagers who do not know what to make of this odd-looking man with his queer ways who has come to live among them. That he does not worship at the parish church is only one of the factors setting him apart from his neighbors, but, significantly, his absorption into the community is paralleled, if not caused, by his increasing involvement in the prevailing religion. This, in turn, takes place through Eppie. He goes to the village church for the first time, at Dolly Winthrop's urging, when Eppie is christened.

He was quite unable, by means of anything he heard or saw, to identify the Raveloe religion with his old faith; if he could at any time in his previous life have done so, it must have been by the aid of a strong feeling ready to vibrate with sympathy, rather than by a comparison of phrases and ideas: and now for long years that feeling had been dormant. He had no distinct idea about the baptism and the church-going, except that Dolly had said it was for the good of the child; and in this way, as the weeks grew to months, the child created fresh and fresh links between his life and the lives from which he had hitherto shrunk continually into narrower isolation (ch. xiv).

Many years later, when he tries to find Lantern Yard, the site and symbol of his early religious experiences, it is gone: so really is the old Silas, whose attitude toward religion had once done so much to keep him from fellowship with those around him.

It is noteworthy that in the four cases I have discussed so far, the religious differences between the intruders and their societies are smoothed over or resolved by the forces of human sympathy and compassion. The admirable qualities of Tryan and Dinah are such that all men of good will must eventually be brought to respect them, even if they do not share them; and when Barton and Silas are struck down by great misfortune, the community, in spite of its former animosity, stands ready to help. The case of Bulstrode in *Middlemarch* (a much later novel), reveals a view of human nature that is neither so simple nor so flattering.

Middlemarch never really does accept Bulstrode. Not only his strict, Evangelical views on theology but also his overbearing manner, his all-powerful position as banker, and, not least, his mysterious origin make him a man to be kept at arm's length by the established members of society and to be feared by the more humble. And when Bulstrode encounters his great crisis, there is no outpouring of compassion from the community. It is the prevailing view in Middlemarch that Bulstrode is not entirely innocent of the death in his house of Raffles, a man whom Bulstrode had excellent reason to want out of the way, and that he has somehow subverted the physician Lydgate to abet this devoutly wished-for consummation. That this paragon of piety has come under a cloud is greeted with something like glee, more or less repressed, by the world of Middlemarch. "The business was felt to be so public and important that it required dinners to feed it, and many invitations were just then issued and accepted on the strength of this scandal concerning Bulstrode and Lydgate; wives, widows, and single ladies took their work and went out to tea oftener than usual; and all public conviviality, from the Green Dragon to Dollop's, gathered a zest which could not be won from the question whether the Lords would throw out the Reform Bill" (ch. lxxi). The discussion at Mrs. Dollop's establishment in Slaughter Lane is no less spirited and a good deal more explicit than the politely shocked conversations which sprang up elsewhere in Middlemarch. As the landlady herself says scornfully,

"But hypo*crite* as he's been, and holding things with that high hand, as there was no parson i' the country good enough for him, he was forced to take Old Harry into his counsel, and Old Harry's been too many for him."

"Ay, ay, he's a 'complice you can't send out o' the country," said Mr. Crabbe the glazier, who gathered much news and groped among it dimly. "But by what I can make out, there's them says Bulstrode was for running away, for fear o' being found out, before now."

"He'll be drove away, whether or no," said Mr. Dill, the barber, who had just dropped in. "I shaved Fletcher, Hawley's clerk, this morning—he's got a bad finger—and he says they're all of one mind to get rid of Bulstrode. Mr. Thesiger is turned against him, and wants him out o' the parish. And there's gentlemen in this town says they'd as soon dine with a fellow from the hulks. 'And a deal sooner I would,' says Fletcher; 'for what's more against one's stomach than a man coming and making himself bad company with his religion, and giving out as the Ten Commandments are not enough

for him, and all the while he's worse than half the men at the tread-mill?'
Fletcher said so himself" (ch. lxxi).

The end is disaster for Bulstrode and his wife: the intruder is repelled.

Religion, however, is not the only basis of conflict between George Eliot's
outsiders and society. In a number of significant cases, they violate accepted
standards of behavior because they are imperceptive, or willful, or driven by
motives which are utterly alien to provincial traditions. They do not know,
or they do not care, that they must alter to fit their new surroundings.

Hetty Sorrel is an interesting early example of this sort of intrusion. An
orphan taken into his home by her Uncle Poyser, the narcissistic Hetty is a
complete misfit in the industrious world of the Hall Farm and the upright
society of Hayslope. She is so totally absorbed in her own vain desires that
she is unable to see the discrepancy between her view of life and that of the
people around her. Hetty's obtuseness plunges her into tragedy and gives the
plot of *Adam Bede* its most powerful forward thrust.

The cases of Harold Transome in *Felix Holt* and Lydgate in *Middlemarch* are perhaps even more interesting. In one sense, of course, Transome
is not an intruder at all. At the beginning of the novel he returns to his boy-
hood home, Transome Court, after fifteen years' absence. But these fifteen
years, which he has spent in business in the Near East, have effected great
changes in him, much to the dismay of his mother, who expects Transome
to slip acquiescently into the life of a country squire and to stand for Parliament as a Conservative. Mrs. Transome notices the physical alteration of her
son immediately, but is much more deeply shocked when, minutes after
their initial greeting, Harold announces that he is no Tory and means to
offer himself as a Radical candidate. After this disturbing beginning, Harold
Transome proceeds relentlessly to unsettle the life of Transome Court, the
estate, the village of Little Treby, and, indeed, the whole constituency of
North Loamshire. The arrival on the scene of this young man so willing
and eager to fly in the face of private and public opinion profoundly affects
the lives and fortunes of every important character in the novel. His insistence on waging the campaign as a Radical and his involvement with the
lawyer Jermyn, who acts as his somewhat reluctant election agent, leads,
directly or indirectly, to the revelation of his true parentage, Esther Lyon's
discovery of her claim to Transome Court, and Felix Holt's grave difficulties
with the law. Of course, it also helps to make possible the outcome of the
romantic plot of the novel, the union between Esther and Felix.

Lydgate, despite the "spots of commonness" which George Eliot takes
pains to point out in his character, is certainly the most sympathetic of the

intruder-figures whom I have treated up to now, and the fact that the world of Middlemarch deals so harshly with him (and Bulstrode) does a great deal to make the novel considerably grimmer than Eliot's earlier studies of provincial life. Lydgate is a man of lofty ideals and aspirations, crammed with advanced Edinburgh and Paris notions, whom his new neighbors simply do not understand. In their limited view, a physician is and ought to be a pill-pusher with a soothing bedside manner, not a scientist interested in research; and Lydgate's novel approach to medical ethics—his refusal to dispense drugs, for instance—arouses suspicion rather than admiration. Although Lydgate's attractive manner speedily secures him a following, the lay public as a whole is as disturbed by this intruder as the doctors and other medical practitioners whose delicately balanced hierarchy he brings into jeopardy with his new ideas. The Rev. Mr. Farebrother's warning to Lydgate is prophetic: "You have not only got the old Adam in yourself against you, but you have got all those descendants of the original Adam who form the society all around you" (ch. xvii). Held back by the dead weight of the Middlemarch girl he has married in his blindness, and frustrated by the incomprehension and hostility of the community, particularly after the Raffles scandal, Lydgate is forced to abandon his plan to carry on research at the New Fever Hospital, and leaves Middlemarch. He does prosper, just as his wife Rosamond hopes and expects he will, but his encounter with Middlemarch has drained all the idealism out of him. Lydgate ends his days ministering to the ailments of the rich, like the physicians at whom he had scoffed in Middlemarch.

Though all George Eliot's physical intruders bring foreign ways and notions into their new environments with them, this is naturally more pronounced in some cases than others. Some of these people are literally foreigners, and their difficulties are likely to be particularly great. The Countess Czerlaski in "Amos Barton" and Will Ladislaw in *Middlemarch* are on the fringes of this group. Both of them are really English but have strong foreign associations: the Countess is the widow of a Polish *émigré* dancing-master; Will is the grandson of another Polish refugee, and has lived much abroad himself. Both of them indulge in what provincial English society considers eccentric behavior, and (although there is some doubt in Shepperton about the Countess' claim to her title) this behavior is all the more vigorously condemned because it is, as Mr. Podsnap would say, "not English."

In "Mr. Gilfil's Love Story," Caterina Sarti is a young Italian girl who has lived with an English county family since infancy. Though all her rearing has been English, certain elements in her character, obviously intended to be typically Latin, nevertheless set her apart from those around her. She is dark in coloring; she is musically gifted, endowed with an excellent voice; she still uses scraps of Italian, particularly terms of endearment; most significantly and fatally, her nature is much more passionate than that of her Anglo-Saxon associates. Caterina loves a Captain Wybrow, and he makes love to her; he has no intention of marrying Caterina, however, and becomes engaged to another young lady. Caterina, we may presume, takes this infidelity much more to heart than a cool English girl would have done: she plans to kill Wybrow, and is only prevented from stabbing him by the fact that he dies of natural causes first. It is Caterina, dagger in hand, who discovers his body. Her remorse is as sharp as her wrath had been, and her sense of guilt casts a permanent blight on her life and her brief marriage to Mr. Gilfil. The plot as I have summarized it (I hope not unfairly), sounds improbable; it would have been impossible if Caterina had been English, which is surely why George Eliot made her Italian.

Tito Melema's situation in *Romola* is much more complicated. The setting is Renaissance Florence and not rural England in the first third of the nineteenth century. Like all human communities, the Midland towns and villages which George Eliot depicts in her English novels are often divided, sometimes deeply, but by contrast with the turbulent Florence of Savonarola and the Medici they seem placid indeed. Milby, Raveloe, or Middlemarch, in a sense, present much more of a united front to an intruder than does fifteenth century Florence. Also, because of the exposed geographical position of his city no sophisticated Florentine could declare with a sniff, as Mrs. Plymdale does in *Middlemarch*, "I should say I was not fond of strangers coming into a town" (ch. xxxi). Strangers came and went daily in Florence: if they were exceptionally charming, clever, energetic, ambitious, and unprincipled, as the Greek Tito was, they could rise to prominence quickly. This was especially true if they were willing, like Tito, to exploit for their own ends the conflicts which were tearing the city apart. An as alien, Tito had no emotional commitment either to the Mediceans, to the Piagnoni (the followers of Savonarola), or to the Compagnacci (a violent aristocratic group opposed to both the other factions). All he cared about was power, and he was willing to throw in his lot with whatever group seemed to him to offer the quickest and surest road to power. If this meant switching his allegiance from one party to another, Tito was quite prepared to do so, and he was adroit enough at times to work secretly with all three opposing parties simultaneously. When his "triple game" grew too complicated even for him to manage, and his own safety was threatened, Tito had no compunctions about betraying his Medicean fellow conspirators to the ruling Piagnoni, even though this brought about the death of his wife's beloved godfather among others. After all, these were not his people: soon "he might turn his back on these hard, eager Florentines, with their futile quarrels and sinking fortunes" (III, xxxvii) and move on in search of new worlds to conquer—at Rome perhaps, or in Milan, in both of which cities Tito had been careful to woo influential friends. Appropriately enough, however, he became inextricably caught up in this web of deceit he had woven, and he met his death while fleeing from a mob of vengeance-seeking Compagnacci. The foreigner who had sought and found "such power as is possible to talent without traditional ties and without beliefs" (II, xix) thus discovered that he could not simply detach himself from his new city and its internecine quarrels, which he had done so much to intensify. The amoral Tito's treachery, public and private, is at the core of the action of *Romola*, and the fact that he is an alien in Florence does much to make that treachery possible.

II

As Barbara Hardy has pointed out in her brilliant study of George Eliot's novels, the most memorable protagonists of these books—Maggie, Romola, Esther, Dorothea, and Gwendolen—"all share the *ex officio* disability of being women" (*The Novels of George Eliot*, p. 47). But it is not only their sex which causes their troubles and allows the critic to consider these characters together. Indeed, I should like to add a man, Daniel Deronda, to the list, and argue that it is their feeling of being ill at ease in their social environments which does most to lend them such kinship as they have. Though the term "intruder" may not be literally applicable to any of them, they are all alienated in one way or another, distressed because the worlds in which they live furnish them no adequate outlets for emotions and impulses which they only half understand.

Maggie Tulliver is perhaps the most extreme case in the earlier novels: a dark, impetuous, imaginative stranger in the fair, comfortable Dodson world of St. Ogg's. As the cripple Philip, himself something of an outcast, recognizes, Maggie's "eyes were full of unsatisfied intelligence, and unsatisfied beseeching affection" (II, v). Neither Maggie's "intelligence" nor her "affection" is ever permanently satisfied in her little world, and its hold on her is too strong to permit her to break away.

Esther Lyon's problems, on the other hand, are of such a nature that they can be settled without much difficulty. As Felix Holt recognizes when he first sees her, she is clearly out of place in Mr. Lyon's house.

She was quite incongruous with his notion of ministers' daughters in general; and though he had expected something nowise delightful, the incongruity repelled him. A very delicate scent, the faint suggestion of a garden, was wafted as she went. He would not observe her, but he had a sense of an elastic walk, the tread of small feet, a long neck and a high crown of shining brown plaits with curls that floated backward,—things, in short, that suggested a fine lady to him, and determined him to notice her as little as possible. A fine lady was always a sort of spun-glass affair,—not natural, and with no beauty for him as art; but a fine lady as the daughter of this rusty old Puritan was especially offensive (ch. v).

But with Felix to act as her mentor, Esther is brought to recognize the vanity and frivolousness of her dreams. She stands by Mr. Lyon; she refuses the chance to be a genuine "fine lady" which the Transomes hold out to her; she accepts Felix. Because she is the least complicated of these intruder-figures, she is able to achieve a more satisfactory adjustment to the conditions of real life than any of the others, with the possible exception of Daniel Deronda.

His situation is comparable to hers because Daniel's feelings of discomfort are also attributable to heredity: like Esther, he does not know who he is. (Esther, it will be remembered, is not really Mr. Lyon's daughter, but the child of an English adventurer and a French mother.) Daniel believes himself to be Sir Hugo Mallinger's natural son, and senses that his position in Sir Hugo's house is somehow odd. Though he is a happy, intelligent, affectionate youngster, on excellent terms with his "uncle," Daniel is afflicted by a "silent consciousness of grief within, which might be compared in some ways with Byron's susceptibility about his deformed foot" (ch. xvi). After he receives "the education of an English gentleman" which Sir Hugo has promised him, his spiritual malaise increases rather than diminishes: there is nothing in the world of an English gentleman that he considers worth doing. It is not until he discovers the truth about his Jewish parentage that Daniel's life takes on genuine meaning. He has, of course, already been introduced to Jewish thought by Mordecai and is deeply attached to Mirah, but it is only when he learns of his own Jewishness that his sympathies and aspirations fall into a coherent pattern: he will work to restore "a political existence to my people, making them a nation again" (ch. lxix)—a mission far different from any of the careers which the well-meaning Sir Hugo has been urging on him.

Dorothea Brooke in *Middlemarch* resembles Daniel in that she too is fired by a sense of mission which is, initially at least, undirected. As George Eliot's famous Prelude reminds us, Dorothea is "a cygnet . . . reared uneasily among the ducklings in the brown pond," a modern St. Theresa whose "passionate, ideal nature demanded an epic life"—a saint without a cause. (It may be remarked in passing that one reason Dorothea is so much more successful as a character than Daniel is that Eliot is able to view Dorothea's yearnings with detachment and occasional irony.) The matter-of-fact milieu of Tipton Grange affords her very little opportunity to fulfill her idealistic dreams, and her mistaken notion that marriage with the pedant Casaubon will not only remove her from this uncongenial environment but allow her "to devote herself to large yet definite duties," "to live continually in the light of a mind that she could reverence" (ch. v), plunges her into disaster.

Dorothea does achieve usefulness, though of a less exalted sort than she had formerly craved, in her second marriage. Reaching such a point of repose at the end of the novel, she is strongly reminiscent of an earlier George Eliot heroine. Romola, though deeply attached to her blind father, does not live up to her potentialities, as a woman or a human being, in catering to the needs of that querulous old scholar. As she waits on him, "it was evident that the deepest fount of feeling within her had not yet wrought its way to the less changeful features, and only found its outlet through her eyes" (I, v). Not until she becomes involved successively with Tito, Savonarola, and the suffering poor of Florence and the nearby plague-stricken village does she play a role in life commensurate with her desires and abilities.

Of this second kind of intruder-figure, the one for whom the reader feels the greatest pity is Gwendolen Harleth, the last in the series. This is so not merely because Gwendolen is left unfulfilled at the end of *Daniel Deronda*, but because her isolation from the beginning is so much more desperate than that of any of these characters. She is not only an outcast in a social group: she is cut off from sympathetic ties with humanity in general by her frigid egotism. Spoiled and intractable from childhood, shunted about for years from one watering place, Parisian apartment, or expensive boarding school to another, Gwendolen finds it difficult to feel close to anyone. She indignantly rejects the conventional girl's notion of a happy life, mindful of her mother's unfortunate second marriage. Gwendolen asks Mrs. Davilow, early in the novel:

"Well, but what is the use of my being charming, if it is to end in my being dull and not minding anything? Is that what marriage always comes to?"

"No, child, certainly not. Marriage is the only happy state for a woman, as I trust you will prove."

"I will not put up with it if it is not a happy state. I am determined to be happy—at least not to go on muddling away my life as other people do, being and doing nothing remarkable. I have made up my mind not to let other people interfere with me as they have done" (ch. iii).

Accordingly, she refuses the pleasant and eminently eligible Rex Gascoigne ("I shall never love anybody. I can't love people. I hate them" [ch. vii]), only to be forced ultimately into a marriage with Grandcourt the vile, who robs her of her most precious possession, her freedom to do as she pleases, and crushes her ego in countless painful ways. She does in due course achieve a kind of communion with Deronda, but on his side at least it is completely lofty and impersonal, and her dimly felt hope that this may grow into a closer relationship is dashed when Daniel leaves her for Mirah, Judaism, and Palestine.

III

One wonders why George Eliot was so strongly drawn to the intruder-figure as the typical mainspring of her plots. To establish links between literature and biography, however tentative, is always perilous, but it may safely be asked whether this unique human being did not look upon her own characteristic role in life as that of an intruder, first in her family's conventional, Evangelical household at Griff, and later in the great world beyond.

Certainly she had ample grounds for viewing herself in this way. The biographical record, such as it is, makes it clear that it was never easy for Mary Ann Evans to feel accepted and comfortable anywhere. Even as a child, loving her family deeply, she lived a solitary existence much of the time. Cross refers to her "pre-eminently exclusive disposition" as a girl (*George Eliot's Life*, I, 11), and she herself wrote to Maria Lewis that "when I was quite a little girl I could not be satisfied with the things around me; I was constantly living in a world of my own creation, and was quite contented to have no companions that I might be left to my own musings and imagine scenes in which I was chief actress" (*Letters*, I, 22). Although Mary Ann Evans continued through adolescence and early adulthood to do her duty to her family as she saw it, her sense of estrangement from her environment persisted and grew. Accordingly, we find her at the age of twenty writing to Miss Lewis that "I begin to feel involuntarily isolated, and without being humble, to have such a consciousness that I am the negation of all that finds love and esteem as makes me anticipate for myself—no matter what; I shall have countless undeserved enemies if my life be prolonged, wherever my sad lot may be cast, and I need rigid discipline, which I have never yet had" (*Letters*, I, 51).

What may be regarded as the climax of this phase of her alienation came sixteen months later, when she refused to accompany her father to church. In a letter which surely wounded him deeply, she announced that she could not unite herself "with any Christian community," that she could not accept "the Divine authority of the books comprising the Jewish and Christian Scriptures." "Such being my very strong convictions, it cannot be a question with any mind of strict integrity, whatever judgment may be passed on their truth, that I could not without vile hypocrisy and a miserable truckling to the smile of the world for the sake of my supposed interests, profess to join in worship which I wholly disapprove" (*Letters*, I, 128-129).

After her departure from Griff, Mary Ann Evans again and again entered new worlds in which, despite encouragement and success of all sorts, she must have felt, at least occasionally, acutely ill at ease. Even the atmosphere of the Brays' circle at Coventry, liberal and tolerant, was certainly something of a shock to one as recently enmeshed in orthodox standards as Mary Ann Evans had been. Later, she could hardly have helped regarding herself as an intruder in John Chapman's bizarre establishment in the Strand; there, and apparently at Dr. Brabant's some time earlier, the other ladies under the roof feared that she might steal the affection of the head of the household and brought about her departure.

In a larger sense, of course, her whole life during the early 1850's was an impertinence: here was a young provincial, a woman at that, wielding immense authority on the *Westminster Review*, the most estimable intellectual publication of the day, mingling on a basis of equality with such eminent figures as Spencer, the Martineaus, Mill, Forster, J. A. Froude, Huxley, and Lewes. And her extra-marital union with George Henry Lewes, though she was able to justify it eloquently and many enlightened spirits stood by her, nevertheless forced Mary Ann Evans into a highly ambiguous position vis-à-vis mid-Victorian society, from which she could not completely extricate herself for a quarter-century. One is tempted to speculate whether her almost constant complaints about ill health (references to these take up two-thirds of a column, in fine print, of Professor Haight's index to the *Letters*), depression, and fatigue did not owe something to a feeling, conscious or subconscious, that she was living in a social world to which she did not really belong.

However that may be, it is not necessary to indulge in psychologizing of this sort to recognize that the intruder-motif plays a prominent part in all of George Eliot's fiction. Although as subtle and massive an *œuvre* as hers can never be explained by any simple "key," the conclusion is inescapable that each of her novels is set, or kept, in motion by the clash between one or more "outsiders" and the social world at large.

Evidence and Testimony: Philip Henry Gosse and the *Omphalos* Theory

by Peter Caws

> Eccentricity has always abounded when and where strength of character has abounded; and the amount of eccentricity in a society has generally been proportional to the amount of genius, mental vigour, and moral courage it contained.
>
> John Stuart Mill, *On Liberty,* ch. III.

I

Eccentricity took many forms in Victorian England, but in keeping with the atmosphere of the times there were two especially noticeable varieties. There were religious eccentrics, like John Nelson Darby, a passionate nonconformist who solved the ancient problem as to the nature of the sin against the Holy Ghost by identifying it with the taking of Holy Orders; and there were scientific eccentrics, like Andrew Crosse, who in the course of electrical experiments at his country estate created a new species of beetle *(Acarus crossii)* and brought down on himself a torrent of totally undeserved abuse on the grounds that he was trying to be God. From time to time these tendencies were combined in a single individual, with invariably interesting results. Religion and science have never really been comfortable in one another's presence, and the antics to which men are driven who try to make them so have not ceased yet. Contemporary attempts, however, seem anaemic in comparison with the fierce controversies of the nineteenth century. What now is done weakly, even pathetically, was then a matter for "genius, mental vigour, and moral courage"; and while the result might have been to make a man look ridiculous, it never made him look puerile. The subject of this essay seems often comic, sometimes tragic, but always a man of strong character and firm will.

Philip Henry Gosse is best known, if at all, as the overbearing Father in Edmund Gosse's autobiographical sketch *Father and Son,* although the sympathies of the reader of that book are likely to lie, as they were intended to lie, with the son. The story is the familiar one: a sickly child, brought up under the stern and repressive eye of a Victorian father, eventually throws off the burden and sets out to live his own life. He was, of course, quite right to do so, and I do not wish to suggest otherwise. My purpose is to draw attention to what Edmund Gosse himself calls "the unique and noble figure of the father"[1]—a distinguished naturalist, author of one of the most brilliant failures in the history of scientific theories, and in his own right a more colorful figure than the son as whose father he himself suspected he would one day be known. He was born in 1810, the son of an itinerant miniature painter, and died in 1888 a Fellow of the Royal Society and the author of more than thirty books and of innumerable scientific papers. It is perhaps best to begin with an account of his scientific development.

At first glance there is nothing eccentric in the professional life of Philip Gosse. Brought up in a small seaport town where the principal form of recreation was exploring the shore or the surrounding country, and spending a great part of his early life in comparatively remote and wild places—first Newfoundland, then Canada, and finally Alabama—it was not surprising that his innate powers of keen observation should have led him into a career as a naturalist. In Newfoundland, where he was employed as a clerk in a whaling office at Carbonear, he bought Kanmacher's edition of Adams's *Essays on the Microscope,* an act which he regarded, in his characteristically self-critical way, as a formal dedication to a life of science. By the time he left Newfoundland for an abortive attempt at farming in Ontario he had already begun an extensive collection of insects which occupied the foreground of his attention; his last memento of Newfoundland was a rare cockroach, and the sole comment in his diary when he first reached Canada was the following: "July 15.—As I this day arrived in Quebec, I procured some lettuce for my caterpillars, which they ate greedily."[2] This single-mindedness in matters of biology remained with him for the rest of his life; the birth of his only child appears in the diary with the entry: "E. delivered of a son. Received green swallow from Jamaica."[3] Of course such things might be interpreted, not unjustly, as indicating a certain stolidity of character, and there is plenty of other evidence to show that Gosse, as a young man, took things very seriously indeed, himself most seriously of all.

The Canadian venture proving a failure, Gosse traveled to Philadelphia (observing en route the rudeness of the natives of Vermont) and there met a number of the leading American naturalists of the period, including members of the remarkable Peale family.[4] From Philadelphia he proceeded, mainly by ship, to Mobile, and thence to King's Landing and Dallas, Alabama, where for nine months he was a schoolmaster. The natives of Alabama were also rude, and they were still extremely anti-English (it was barely sixty years since the Revolution); and although Philip Gosse enjoyed many things about his stay in the South, including the "woffles" which were served

GOSSE AND THE *Omphalos* THEORY

for breakfast, the frequent violence, especially towards the Negroes, and
the almost tangible moral strain of slavery, made him glad to leave and
return to England after twelve years in the Americas.[5]

It was not easy to find suitable work in England, and for the first year
after his return Gosse lived in something close to penury. He spent some
time, however, in working the notes of his Canadian period into a manuscript entitled *The Canadian Naturalist,* a series of imaginary conversations,
somewhat stiff in tone, between a father and son, on the flora and fauna of
the region in which he had stayed. At first he met with no success in finding
a publisher, but finally, when he was at "the extremity of dejection and dis-
gust," he was sent for by Mr. John Van Voorst of Paternoster Row. Edmund
Gosse describes the interview:

The publisher began slowly: "I like your book; I shall be pleased to publish
it; I will give you one hundred guineas for it." One hundred guineas! It
was Peru and half the Indies! The reaction was so violent that the demure
and ministerial looking youth, closely buttoned up in his worn broadcloth,
broke down utterly into hysterical sob upon sob, while Mr. Van Voorst, mur-
muring, "My dear young man! My dear young man!" hastened out to fetch
wine and minister to wants which it was beyond the power of pride to
conceal any longer.[6]

This was the beginning of a long association between author and publisher.
The Canadian Naturalist showed what he could do in a literary direction,
and as time went on he learned to do it brilliantly. He could be erudite and
familiar at the same time, interspersing careful zoological and botanical
observations with amusing anecdotes, providing his own illustrations in
line or watercolor, and turning out, over the next thirty-five years, a dozen
or more enormously successful books of popular natural history. He ac-
quired a large and faithful public, which enthusiastically bought his books
and took them to the seaside, despoiling in the process (much to his chagrin)
the shore which was his favorite collecting-ground. Gosse's relation to his
readers is perfectly foreshadowed in the relation between the father and the
son in *The Canadian Naturalist.* The father, in the opening chapter of that
book, proposes a series of excursions into the neighbouring countryside:
"Charles.—Few things would give me greater pleasure. I have often felt
the want of a companion in my walks, who, by his superior judgement,
information, and experience, might remove my doubts, gratify my curiosity,
and direct my attention to those subjects which are instructive as well as
amusing; for I anticipate both instruction and amusement from our inquiries,
and enter into your proposal with delight."[7] The genteel sections of the

71

Victorian middle classes were equally delighted, and were instructed and amused in the thousands not only by Gosse's books but also by his invention of the aquarium, which brought the seashore into drawing-rooms all over the country.

Scientific work of a more serious nature was not, however, neglected. Gosse crossed the Atlantic once more for a two-year study of the birds of Jamaica, which produced one of the important early works on the ornithology of the West Indies. His inflexible uprightness of character is illustrated by an incident in connection with the publication of a supplement to that work, the *Illustrations of the Birds of Jamaica,* a rare and exceedingly beautiful set of colored plates each bearing the inscription "P.H.G. del. et lith." These were published by subscription, and in the course of printing it became apparent that the cost of production would exceed the total amount subscribed; but rather than change the price of the work once announced, Gosse absorbed the extra cost out of his own pocket, actually publishing the set at a loss. Subsequent studies, especially of small and microscopic forms of marine life, led to his election to the Royal Society in 1856. Darwin corresponded with him, asking for information in connection with his own painstaking work on variation, and he was honored by being taken into the confidence of the biological revolutionaries of the 1850's:

It was the notion of Lyell . . . that before the doctrine of natural selection was given to a world which would be sure to lift up at it a howl of execration, a certain body-guard of sound and experienced naturalists, expert in the description of species, should be privately made aware of its tenour. Among those who were thus initiated, or approached with a view towards possible illumination, was my Father. He was spoken to by Hooker, and later on by Darwin, after meetings of the Royal Society in the summer of 1857.[8]

Gradually his interest became concentrated in a few highly specialized areas, particularly the Rotifera, and he wrote one classic of nineteenth-century zoology, the *Actinologia Britannica,* which remained the standard reference work for many years. He was an indefatigable observer, and cannot really be said to have retired at all; at the age of seventy-five he was still busily occupied, publishing in 1885 a monograph on *The Prehensile Armature of the Papillonidae.*

Gosse's great merit as a scientist lay in a capacity, rarely encountered, for precision and minuteness in observation, which called for extraordinary resources of patience and eyesight, neither of which seems ever to have failed him in connection with his scientific work. In *The Birds of Jamaica* he enunciates a principle to which he always adhered and which is of supreme importance in the descriptive branches of science:

Perhaps a word of apology may be thought needful for the minuteness with which the author has sometimes recorded dates, and other apparently trivial circumstances, in his observations. It is because of his conviction, that an observer is hardly competent to determine what circumstance is trivial, and what is important: many a recorded fact in science has lost half its value from the omission of some attendant circumstance, which the observer either did not notice or thought irrelevant. It is better to err on the side of minuteness than of vagueness.[9]

When, at rare intervals, he allowed himself to wander from this close attention to the facts, the results were, from a scientific point of view, less happy. His speculations, largely on the question of the creation and extinction of species (although he also put forward the theory that some frequently reported sea serpents were really prehistoric monsters) were generally naïve, while his taste, left to its own devices, ran in the direction of the Gothic novel. The subtitles of that most romantic work, *The Romance of Natural History,* show the scientist in an entirely different light. Chapter X, entitled "The Terrible" (other chapters are called "The Vast," "The Wild," "The Unknown"), deals with the following surprising collection of incidents: "Horrible Death of Thackwray—Hottentot's Adventure with a Rhinoceros—Similar Adventure of Mr. Oswell—Terrific Peril of Captain Methuen—Nearly Fatal Combat with a Kangaroo—Horrid Voracity of Sharks—Coolness of an Indian Officer—Ugliness of Vipers—Shocking Adventure in Guiana—Another in Venezuela—Fatal Encounter with Bees in India." The last of these episodes has, for this study, a special interest. It concerns two English gentlemen, Messrs. Armstrong and Boddington; the victim, inevitably, was "alas! Mr. Boddington," who "unable any longer to resist the countless hordes of his infuriated winged foes, threw himself into the depths of the water, never to rise again." Gosse is not actually sure that the assailants were bees, and covers his admission of ignorance with this remarkable statement: "Whatever the true nature of the insect, it affords an apt illustration of such passages of Holy Scripture as the following:—'The Lord shall hiss for . . . the bee that is the land of Assyria,' (Isa. vii. 18.) 'The Lord thy God will send the hornet among them, until they that are left, and hide themselves from thee, be destroyed.' (Deut. vii. 20.)"[10]

Overlooking for the moment the claim to aptness (from whom was Mr. Boddington hiding? and why Assyria?), here is a strange insertion into the work of a Fellow of the Royal Society. But by this time, after twenty years, anybody familiar with Gosse's writings would have taken it in his stride. Wherever one looks one finds passing confessions of faith, references to the Bible, exhortations to the young, and while these might at first be taken for customary piety, the weight of the evidence, and the recondite nature of some of the allusions (such as those in the case of Mr. Boddington) soon suggest a different hypothesis. It is impossible to do justice to the life and work of Philip Gosse without paying close attention to this other side of his character.

II

When Philip Gosse returned to England from America in 1839, urgently in need of employment, he was offered a post in a provincial museum. He was hardly in a position to be particular about conditions of work, and the offer was really an act of charity on the part of an interested friend, but he turned it down.

> I should fear [he wrote] that I should be thrown into situations in which I might find it difficult to keep that purity of intention which I value more than life; and likewise, that my opportunities of being useful to my fellow-men, especially to their souls, would be much curtailed. I view this transient state as a dressing-room to a theatre; a brief, almost momentary visit, during which preparation is to be made for the real business and end of existence. Eternity is our theatre: time our dressing-room. So that I *must* make every arrangement with a view to its bearing on this one point.[11]

Apparently he was entertaining, at this time, the idea of entering the ministry of one of the evangelical sects. But he could hardly be said to have been brought up in a religious atmosphere. For the origin of this pious tendency it is necessary to go back to Newfoundland, and to the time, almost exactly, of his purchase of Adams on the microscope—a time at which he "became, suddenly and consciously, a naturalist and a Christian."[12] The stimulus for his conversion, if it can be called that, was an illness of his sister Elizabeth, far away in England, to whom he was closely attached. "My prominent thought in this crisis was legal. I wanted the Almighty to be my friend; to go to Him in my need. I know He required me to be holy. He had said, 'My son, give Me thy heart.' I closed with Him, not hypocritically, but sincerely; intending henceforth to live a new, a holy life; to please and serve God."[13] It was as if he had signed a contract with God; and it did not occur to him to doubt, since he knew himself to be strong enough in character to keep his part of the bargain, that God would in turn do what was expected of Him.

This contract of faith he interpreted as requiring the acceptance, word for word, of the literal and symbolic truth of the Bible. The double sense is important. While the plain meaning of the text was to be zealously defended, there was more to be discovered beneath the surface. Gosse applied himself to the investigation of this hidden truth with an energy matched only by that which he devoted to his researches in natural history. At first these studies were carried on in comparative isolation, but after his return to England two circumstances mitigated this spiritual loneliness. He found, in the suburb of London where he was for a short time a schoolmaster, a group of Christians, followers of J. N. Darby, called by the outside world "Plymouth Brethren" but by themselves simply "the Brethren," or, modestly, "the Saints." Darby, as was remarked earlier, disapproved of the ministry, so that Gosse was no longer tempted in that direction; but he found among these people a kind of intellectual interest in salvation and prophecy perfectly in sympathy with his own convictions. He was, throughout his life, evangelical, but never in the passionate sense usually attached to the word. His concern for the souls of men sprang less from sympathy than from duty, and the duty was not necessarily pleasant—it was part of the agreement with God, a service demanded in exchange for the right to enter into the mysteries of the interpretation of Scripture. Independently of this connection he met, and later married, Emily Bowes, the daughter of a Bostonian couple, her principal attraction being an equally fervid, equally rigid, and equally eccentric form of Christianity with his own. Together they read the prophets and commentaries on the prophets, treading eagerly, in the words of Edmund Gosse, "the curious path which they had hewn for themselves through this jungle of symbols."[14] The death of his first wife after only nine years of marriage left him, if anything, more isolated than before (the Saints proving too tame and unimaginative for his fierce symbolic tastes), and drove his already rather stern and humorless character into a melancholia from which he never completely recovered.

It was inevitable that such exclusive and fanatic attention to the details of biblical exegesis should before long produce a distorting effect on Gosse's attitude to the contemporary world and, eventually, to science itself. The commentators were, if anything, more prophetic than the prophets, and led the inquisitive couple "to recognise in wild Oriental visions direct statements regarding Napoleon III and Pope Pius IX and the King of Piedmont, historic figures which they conceived as foreshadowed, in language which admitted of plain interpretation, under the names of denizens of Babylon and com-

NINETEENTH-CENTURY STUDIES

panions of the Wild Beast."[15] The Church of Rome in particular figured largely in the deciphering of the Book of Revelation, and it was denounced and hated with a special passion. "We welcomed any social disorder in any part of Italy, as likely to be annoying to the Papacy. If there was a custom-house officer stabbed in a *fracas* at Sassari, we gave loud thanks that liberty and light were breaking in upon Sardinia. . . ."[16] The effects of all this were felt in the most unlikely quarters. There was, for instance, a man who used to pass down the street where the Gosses lived selling onions, with a cry of

> Here's your rope
> To hang the Pope
> And a penn'orth of cheese to choke him.

The cheese [writes Edmund Gosse] appeared to be legendary; he sold only onions. My Father did not eat onions, but he encouraged this terrible fellow, with his wild eyes and long strips of hair, because of his "godly attitude towards the Papacy."[17]

Such peculiarities might have been merely amusing, had they confined themselves to international affairs. But scriptural theory found other applications closer to home, and Philip Gosse developed, out of a naturally strong moral sense and a tendency to introspection, a morbid sensitivity of conscience and a practice of hypercritical self-vigilance which he did not hesitate to extend to his family (principally Edmund) and to the congregation of which, after the death of his wife and his removal to Devonshire, he became informally the pastor. This side of his character is so well known from *Father and Son* that there is no need to dwell on it here. The introduction of religious conviction into daily life produced, however, another effect of more direct interest, namely a relation between the scientist and his field of study perhaps unique in the history of science among workers of comparable distinction.

Nature was the work of God, and as such was to be taken seriously. It must, as the work of God, be perfect. Accordingly, for Gosse, the suggestion that anything in Nature might have been better arranged, or the slightest hint of levity in connection with it, were almost comparable to blasphemy, and he was ready to meet either with indignation on God's behalf. In *The Ocean,* for example, he scornfully rejects a tentative version of the theory of development: "Goldsmith flippantly asserts, that the Shrimp and the Prawn 'seem to be the first attempts which Nature made when she meditated the formation of the Lobster.' Such expressions as these, however, are no less un-philosophical than they are derogatory to God's honour; these animals being

76

in an equal degree perfect in their kind, equally formed by consummate wisdom, incapable of improvement. . . ."[18] But there was a danger in thus zealously guarding God's rights in Nature—the danger that he might, as time went on, come to take a certain proprietary attitude towards it himself; and to this temptation he soon succumbed. He felt fully justified in doing so, and would have been surprised and indignant, as religious people tend to be, if anybody had pointed out to him that to presume on God's favor was a form of spiritual pride. But there is no doubt that Philip Gosse was both proud and presumptuous, and in the *Devonshire Coast* there is a remarkable juxtaposition of passages which form such a clear basis for this indictment that I shall, at the risk of tedium, quote them extensively. He is discussing the aesthetic qualities of natural objects:

But there is another point of view from which a Christian . . . looks at the excellent and the beautiful in Nature. He has a personal interest in it all; *it is a part of his own inheritance.* As a child roams over his father's estate, and is ever finding some quiet nook, or clear pool, or foaming waterfall, some lofty avenue, some bank of sweet flowers, some picturesque or fruitful tree, some noble and widespread prospect,—how is the pleasure heightened by the thought ever recurring,—All this will be *mine* by and by! . . . So with the Christian. . . .

And thus I have a right to examine, with as great minuteness as I can bring to the pleasant task, consistently with other claims, what are called the works of nature. I have the very best right possible, the right that flows from the fact of their being all mine,—mine not indeed in possession, but in sure reversion. And if anyone despise the research as mean and little, I reply that I am scanning the plan of my inheritance. And when I find any tiny object rooted to the rock, or swimming in the sea, in which I trace with more than common measure the grace and delicacy of the Master Hand, I may not only give Him praise for his skill and wisdom, but thanks also, for that He hath taken the pains to contrive, to fashion, to adorn this, *for me.*

And then there follows immediately this statement:

THE CRYSTALLINE JOHNSTONELLA

I have the pleasure of announcing a new animal of much elegance, which I believe to be of a hitherto unrecognised form. I shall describe it under the appellation of *Johnstonella Catharina.* . . .

The elegant form, the crystal clearness, and the sprightly, graceful movements of this little swimmer in the deep sea, render it a not altogether unfit vehicle for the commemoration of an honoured name in marine zoology. . . . I venture respectfully to appropriate to this marine animal, the surname and Christian name of Mrs. Catharine Johnston, as a personal tribute of gratitude for the great aid which I have derived from her engravings in the study of zoophytology.[19]

NINETEENTH-CENTURY STUDIES

Of course it is, in a sense, unfair to put the matter in this way, and to suggest a patronizing flourish in this innocent piece of nomenclature; but there is some justice in it. Ever since that day when, in Newfoundland, he had come to terms with God, Philip Gosse had, consciously or not, felt himself in a position of privilege. Nothing illustrates this attitude more clearly than the nature of his prayers.

Edmund Gosse has vividly described how his father, with clenched fists and cracking fingers, knelt nightly and wrestled with God, his supplications occasionally turning into outright demands. From other sources we can gather what the objects of those demands were. There were three things during his life that Philip Gosse wanted very badly indeed, and to which he expressly devoted a great deal of his spiritual energy in prayer; and in the end, to all appearances, God failed to live up to his commitments, for none of the three requests was granted. The first, and most persistent, was inspired by his reading, as a young man, Habershon's *Dissertation on the Prophetic Scriptures,* in which the Second Coming of Christ was vividly anticipated; in his own words: "I immediately began a practice, which I have pursued uninterruptedly for forty-six years, of constantly praying that I may be one of the favoured saints who shall never taste of death, but be alive and remain until the coming of the Lord, to be 'clothed upon with my house which is from heaven.' "[20] This is not an infrequent prayer among evangelical Christians, who in general, however, seem content to die without a feeling of having been cheated. Not so Philip Gosse. Even in life his confidence was such that he lived in momentary expectation of this apotheosis, and would be chagrined when it did not occur: "He would calculate, by reference to prophecies in the Old and New Testament, the exact date of this event; the date would pass, without the expected Advent, and he would be more than disappointed,—he would be incensed. Then he would understand that he must have made some slight error in calculation, and the pleasures of anticipation would recommence."[21] But at death it was not a question of miscalculation. His second wife, Eliza Gosse (née Brightwen), wrote in a short memoir that "this hope of being caught up before death continued to the last, and its non-fulfilment was an acute disappointment to him. It undoubtedly was connected with the deep dejection of his latest hours on earth."[22]

The second prayer concerned his son, Edmund, and was of especial importance to him as incorporating the last wish of his first wife. Philip and Emily Gosse had, from the beginning, dedicated their child, like Samuel, to the service of the Lord; and Emily, dying of cancer in 1857, reiterated that dedication in the most solemn and saintly manner possible, so that God himself, it seemed, must be bound to accept it and ensure its consummation. For many years all was well, and when Edmund was publicly baptized and admitted to the communion of the Brethren at the age of twelve Philip Gosse felt the sacred responsibility to be almost discharged. But in truth Edmund had hardly known what he was doing, or that any other life than that among the Brethren was conceivable, and when he went to London as a young man to work in the British Museum he discovered that his tastes and talents lay in other directions. Gradually severing his links with the Evangelical Movement, he entered upon a career as a man of letters. Philip Gosse wrote angrily to his son and prayed angrily to his Maker, but in vain.

There remains one episode out of the three in Philip Gosse's life of prayer. It was of shorter duration, but its implications were of vastly greater scope, and its historical interest is such that it will be dealt with in a section by itself.

III

Protestant Christianity, as Martineau somewhere remarks, is built upon the authority of the Bible, as Catholicism is built upon that of the Church. The vulnerability of the first position, as compared with the flexibility of the second, is obvious; for the Church can discreetly change its mind, while the Bible, as a historical document, is by definition incapable of adapting to novelty. Catholicism survived the nineteenth century much better, in its own sphere of influence, than Protestantism did, for this very reason; for in that century more than in any other the intellectual sympathies of the world were alienated from the Bible by the exposure of many apparently straightforward statements of fact in it as ignorant legends. The blow was not, of course, mortal. Ignorant people continued to believe the legends, and the intellectuals began to treat them as mythical adumbrations of profound truths. But those few really educated men to whom the Bible had been genuinely and directly authoritative experienced a most disturbing conflict of loyalties. Philip Gosse is a perfect example of the type.

The greatest problem before 1858, when Darwin and Wallace brought out into the open the question of the origin of species, was geological. According to Archbishop Ussher's reading of Genesis there could not, in 1857 (the year in which Gosse published his own work on the subject), be anything in the world more than 5,861 years old; according to rapidly accumulating stratigraphical and paleontological evidence there was scarcely anything of interest in the world whose history was not much longer than that by hundreds of thousands, even millions, of years. The stratigraphy might be accommodated, at a stretch, by introducing that famous gap of aeons between the first and second verses of Genesis 1, but this did not help the paleontology, especially that of species closely related to living ones, even identical with them. The "days" of creation might be extended to cover geological ages, but there were difficulties there about the order of appearance of fossils in the stratigraphical record, and besides, to the purists, this seemed already to be taking hardly permissible liberties with the manifest declarations of the Holy Spirit. These were grave perplexities for those "to whom," in Gosse's own words,

the veracity of God is as dear as life. They cannot bear to see it impugned; they know that it cannot be overthrown; they are assured that He who gave the Word, and He who made the worlds, is One Jehovah, who cannot be inconsistent with Himself. But they cannot shut their eyes to the startling fact, that the records which *seem* legibly written on His created works do flatly contradict the statements which *seem* to be plainly expressed in His word.

Here is a dilemma. A most painful one to the reverent mind! And many reverent minds have laboured long and hard to escape from it.[23]

Most of them gave up the struggle, either closing their eyes to the evidence, or abandoning the literal interpretation of the Bible, or in many cases just learning to live with the dilemma as something too great for the limited intelligence of man. This last was at least a humble, if not a comfortable, position. But none of this would do for Philip Gosse; he would be content with nothing less than a complete solution of the riddle. The incredible thing is that he succeeded in finding one so perfect that it was, and remains, proof against all refutation. And although he called the book in which he presented it to the world "an attempt to untie the geological knot," his method has all the audacity of Alexander at Gordium.

It was this book, *Omphalos*,[24] whose acceptance by the world of science formed the object of Gosse's third petition to God. His own attitude towards it is made explicit in the preface:

I would not be considered an opponent of geologists; but rather as a co-searcher with them after that which they value as highly as I do, TRUTH. The path which I have pursued has led me to a conclusion at variance with theirs. I have a right to expect that it be weighed; let it not be imputed to vanity if I hope that it may be accepted.

But what I much more ardently desire is, that the thousands of thinking persons, who are scarcely satisfied with the extant reconciliations of Scriptural statements and Geological deductions,—who are silenced but not convinced,— may find, in the principle set forth in this volume, a stable resting-place. I have written it in the constant prayer that the God of Truth will deign so to use it; and if He do, to Him be all the glory![25]

That God *would* deign to use it, given the irresistible force of the argument, seemed beyond all doubt.

Never was a book cast upon the waters [writes Edmund Gosse] with greater anticipation of success than was this curious, this obstinate, this fanatical volume. My Father lived in a fever of suspense, waiting for the tremendous issue. . . . My Father, and my Father alone, possessed the secret of the enigma; he alone held the key which could smoothly open the lock of geological mystery. He offered it, with a glowing gesture, to atheists and Christians alike. This was to be the universal panacea; this the system of intellectual therapeutics which could not but heal all the maladies of the age. But, alas! atheists and Christians alike looked at it and laughed, and threw it away.[26]

In this the Christians, at least, were ill-advised; but at all events the reception of the book meant that here too Gosse's prayers had failed to find a response. Had he known at the time, as he did not, of the two other great disappointments that were in store for him, it might well have broken his spirit; as it was, coming soon after the death of his wife, the failure of *Omphalos* had a sufficiently disturbing effect. But it is time to examine the theory itself. Gillispie says that it was "far from original," and Gosse himself admits that he got the germ of the idea, partly from an anonymous tract, and partly from Granville Penn's *The Mineral and Mosaic Geologies* of 1822. Nevertheless its working out in *Omphalos* and the detail with which its application is followed through bear Gosse's individual mark.

The book is an account of an imaginary court inquiry, with witnesses. One curious thing about it is that, except at the very end, there is no appeal to the Bible; and as for Archbishop Ussher, he is not once mentioned. The whole tone of the book, in fact, is modern, and with one or two critical exceptions there is nothing in it which could not have been accepted by the most hardened atheistic geologist of the time. The case for the geological ages is presented fully, even sympathetically, as the testimony of "The Witness for the Macro-Chronology"; strata, fossils of plants and animals, erosion—all the available evidence is brought out. There are two examples chosen for special attention: the pterodactyl (illustrated by an unintentionally humorous woodcut of a bat with bulging eyes and gaping fangs) and the

Jurassic tree *Lepidodendron*. But when all the data have been marshalled, Gosse puts his finger skilfully on the Achilles heel of the whole argument: ". . . there is nothing here but *circumstantial* evidence; there is no *direct* testimony. . . . You will say, 'It is the same thing; we have seen the skeleton of the one, and the crushed trunk of the other, and therefore we are as sure of their past existence as if we had been there at the time.' No, it is not the same thing; it is not *quite* the same thing; NOT QUITE. . . . It is only by a process of reasoning that you infer they lived at all."[27] Of course he is quite right; the inference of causes from effects commits a logical fallacy. Sciences which deal with the past, or with the unobservable of any kind, constantly commit it—they have no alternative. This fact is tacitly admitted, and then quite properly forgotten, as far as the daily work of the scientist is concerned. But when somebody like Gosse gleefully draws attention to it there is absolutely nothing that can be brought forward in its defense—the only recourse is a challenge to the critic to produce an alternative, and equally plausible, explanation of the effects as they appear. Such a challenge Gosse was quite prepared to meet.

His own theory invokes two postulates, the creation of matter and the persistence of species. "I assume that at some period or other in past eternity there existed nothing but the Eternal God, and that He called the universe into being out of nothing. I demand also, in opposition to the development hypothesis, the perpetuity of specific characters, from the moment when the respective creatures were called into being, till they cease to be."[28] As a matter of fact the second postulate is superfluous—Gosse's theory, while it certainly removes the necessity for a theory of development (or of variation and natural selection), is not incompatible with such a theory. And as for the first, although he refuses to discuss it, nobody was in a position to maintain that there was any better account available of the origin of the universe, assuming that it had an origin. At least the Christians could accept the point without difficulty. Now creation is generally taken to be a beginning of history, and thereby also of natural history—the first verse of Genesis makes the idea explicit. It certainly is a beginning in some sense, but Gosse's reflections led him to see that it could not be so in the way in which, for example, birth is. Birth is the beginning of a phase, but it depends on an earlier phase, namely prenatal development, whereas creation must be an absolute beginning *de novo,* depending upon no antecedents whatever except the will of the Creator. Suppose a creator setting about the creation of some natural object, a fern, a butterfly, a cow; at what stage of its existence should he choose to call it into being? We might unthinkingly choose the mature form; but is there any reason why this should be preferred to an immature or embryonic form? Is any stage fundamentally more suitable than any other as a starting-point of natural history? Gosse concluded not—indeed that there is no such thing as a natural beginning of this necessarily ultimate sort, the court of nature being, in fact, circular. "It is evident that there is no one point in the history of any single creature, which is a legitimate beginning of existence. . . . The cow is as inevitable a sequence of the embryo, as the embryo is of the cow."[29] Such a beginning must, therefore, be supernatural. "Creation, the sovereign fiat of Almighty Power, gives us the commencing point, which we in vain seek in nature. But what is creation? It is *the sudden bursting into a circle.*"[30] And just as the life-cycle of the individual is closed upon itself, so the cycle of species, of life itself, of the planet and the solar and stellar systems, may in principle be ever repeating, from eternity to eternity, only to be commenced or terminated by an irruption from without.

Gosse's stroke of genius thus lay in separating the question of creation from the question of history altogether. The older view has its classical expression in Donne: "That then this Beginning *was,* is matter of faith, and so, infallible. *When* it was, is matter of *reason,* and therefore various and perplex't."[31] Gosse brought it all into the province of faith by suggesting the possibility that natural objects might be created *with a history,* or at least with the appearance of one. And this suggestion, once made, ceased to be a suggestion and became an indispensable necessity: a natural object could not be a natural object without an apparent history. A tree would not be a tree without rings, which indicate its age, and even a newly created tree must have rings. A man would not be a man without a navel, Sir Thomas Browne to the contrary notwithstanding.

The whole organisation of the creature thus newly called into existence, looks back to the course of an endless circle in the past. Its whole structure displays a series of developments, which as distinctly witness to former conditions as do those which are presented in the cow, the butterfly, and the fern, of the present day. But what former conditions? The conditions thus witnessed unto, as being necessarily implied in the present organisation, were non-existent; the history was a perfect blank till the moment of creation. The past conditions or stages of existence in question, can indeed be as triumphantly inferred by legitimate deduction from the present, as can those of our cow or butterfly; they rest on the very same evidences; they are identically the same in every respect, except in this one, that they were *unreal.* They exist only in their results; they are effects which never had causes.

Perhaps it may help to clear my argument if I divide the past developments of organic life, which are necessarily, or at least legitimately, inferrible from present phenomena, into two categories, separated by the violent act of creation. Those unreal developments whose apparent results are seen in the organism at the moment of its creation, I will call *prochronic,* because time was not an element in them; while those which have subsisted since creation, and have had actual existence, I will distinguish as *diachronic,* as occurring during time.

Now, again I repeat, there is no imaginable difference to sense between the prochronic and diachronic development....[32]

Natural history thus appears as an unbroken progression, from some unimaginable beginning in the mind of God to the state of the world at present; somewhere in between an extrinsic act of creation occurred, and as prochronic events ceased, diachronic ones—identical in every essential point—began. When did this take place? Is there any way of deducing it from the evidence? Obviously not: "The commencement, as a fact, I must learn from testimony; I have no means whatever of inferring it from phenomena."[33] Fortunately the testimony is available. God need not have told us when the Creation occurred, but as a matter of fact he has done so, in Genesis, and it would be ungrateful—not to say foolish or even impious—in men of science to overlook the fact. So far they have "not allowed for the Law of Prochronism in Creation,"[34] but without it all calculation is useless; "the amount of error thus produced we have no means of knowing; much less of eliminating it."[35] Accordingly every scrap of evidence for the Macro-Chronology contains a fatal flaw; and, as Gosse triumphantly concludes: "The field is left clear and undisputed for the one Witness on the opposite side, whose testimony is as follows:—

" 'IN SIX DAYS JEHOVAH MADE HEAVEN AND EARTH, THE SEA, AND ALL THAT IN THEM IS.' "[36]

But what, after all, did this victory amount to? To begin with, it showed that there had never really been a struggle: "I do not know that a single conclusion, now accepted, would need to be given up, except that of actual chronology. And even in respect of this, it would be rather a modification than a relinquishment of what is at present held; we might still speak of the inconceivably long duration of the processes in question, provided we understand *ideal* instead of actual time;—that the duration was projected in the mind of God, and not really existent."[37] Reduced to this, the conclusion is merely metaphysical, that is to say empirically empty; to assert that the world was created is rather like asserting that overnight everything in it has doubled in size, including rulers and retinae—nobody can tell the difference. One might as well retort that really everything has halved in size, or that everything has been uncreated, the former existence being real and the present ideal, for all that any experiment can possibly indicate to the contrary. Put in another way, Gosse's claim comes to the same thing as maintaining that, before creation, Berkeley's philosophical position was the correct one, while after it Locke's was. Unfortunately most men persisted in seeing more in it than that, continuing to believe that there was a genuine difference of opinion between the geologists and the Holy Ghost, that it was impossible to agree with both but that it mattered which one agreed with. Gosse was undoubtedly right—it did not matter, at least not in the way that most men supposed, since (apart from the extra-scientific point of faith) one *could* agree with both; but few could follow his intellectual maneuvers, perfectly rational though they were.

And then any victory, even the most conclusive, becomes hollow when nobody takes the slightest notice of it, or when the few who do misinterpret it completely. Having instructed the printers to prepare an unusually large edition of his book against what he was certain would be a universal demand, Gosse found himself in possession of most of it, while the few copies that went out produced a critical reaction of a totally unexpected sort. The theory of *Omphalos,* after suitable distortion—not only by the malicious— became monstrous, asserting nothing less than that God had placed fossils in the rocks for the express purpose of deceiving scientists into thinking that the earth was older than it really was. Perhaps the cruelest blows were struck by that perpetually well-meaning, infallibly clumsy Victorian, Charles Kingsley.

We have reason to be grateful for Kingsley's blunt insensitivity, which produced, like the irritating specks of sand in oysters, responses of great beauty in diverse quarters—the two most famous cases are, of course, Newman's *Apologia pro Vita sua* and Huxley's celebrated letter on the death of his son. There is no record of a similar reaction on Gosse's part, but the stimulus was certainly no less painful. The theory itself, it is true, was perfectly acceptable to Kingsley: "Your distinction between diachronism and prochronism [he wrote to Gosse], instead of being nonsense, as it is in the eyes of the Locke-beridden Nominalist public, is to me, as a Platonist and realist, an indubitable and venerable truth."[38] But Gosse's use of the theory to justify the geologists in the form, if not the substance, of their conclusions, while at the same time preserving the literal truth of Scripture, was too much for him. "Your book tends to prove this—that if we accept the fact of absolute creation, God becomes a *Deus quidam deceptor*. . . . You make God tell a lie. It is not my reason, but my conscience which revolts here."[39] Such obtuseness was bad enough—for Gosse's whole point had been to show that God had not lied at all, that indeed he had been scrupulously honest (as Gosse himself would have been in similar circumstances), correcting in one mode of communication, namely Biblical revelation, a possible misconception which might arise in the interpretation of a message in another mode, namely geological evidence—but there was worse to come. Kingsley, self-confident as ever, went on:

I cannot give up the painful and slow conclusion of five and twenty years' study of geology, and believe that God has written on the rocks one enormous and superfluous lie for all mankind.

To this painful dilemma you have brought me, and will, I fear, bring hundreds. It will not make me throw away my Bible. I trust and hope. I know in whom I have believed, and can trust Him to bring my faith safe through this puzzle, as He has through others; but for the young I do fear. I would not for a thousand pounds put your book into my children's hands. . . . Your demand on implicit faith is just as great as that required for transubstantiation, and, believe me, many of your arguments, especially in the opening chapter, are strangely like those of the old Jesuits, and those one used to hear from John Henry Newman fifteen years ago, when he, copying the Jesuits, was trying to undermine the grounds of all rational belief and human science, in order that, having made his victims (among whom were some of my dearest friends) believe nothing, he might get them by a "Nemesis of faith" to believe anything, and rush blindfold into superstition. Poor wretch, he was caught in his own snare. . . .[40]

Bitter words for a supporter of the onion man! and especially bitter the remark about children, for whose mental and moral improvement Gosse, in his popular writings, had been so solicitous. But then Kingsley and Gosse were fundamentally at cross purposes in this matter. Kingsley's aversion for Rome was intellectual, Gosse's emotional; Gosse's interest in religion and science was intellectual, Kingsley's sentimental. The comparison of Gosse and Newman, ghastly and inconceivable as it would have seemed to them both, was not in fact entirely unjust, for Newman, in the *Apologia,* says: "From the age of fifteen, dogma has been the fundamental principle of my religion: I know no other religion; I cannot enter into the idea of any other sort of religion; religion, as a mere sentiment, is to me a dream and a mockery"[41]—in which substituting for "dogma" "the infallibility of the Scriptures" renders Gosse's belief exactly. Both Newman and Gosse had seen that the defense of truth on the highest level leads sometimes to an appearance of deception on a lower, and both had been reprimanded for it by Kingsley, to whom truth was a simple, straightforward, rather typically English sort of thing.

Newman, however, was the better off; for the Church provides an environment friendly to such subtleties, let infidels protest as they may; but what is a lonely Protestant to do, when God refuses to look after his own interests, and allows his shortsighted and enthusiastic servants to spoil the work of those who are more perceptive and austere? Nothing could shake Gosse's faith in the Bible, but its author, engaged as he was in guiding the Kingsleys of the world safely through their puzzles, might perhaps be guilty of negligence. In his reaction to the failure of *Omphalos* Gosse almost suspected as much. "I think there was added to his chagrin with all his fellow mortals a first tincture of that heresy which was to attack him later on. It was now that, I fancy, he began, in his depression, to be angry with God."[42] But this was not the petulant anger of a disappointed scholar. It is exactly here that Gosse's enormous intellectual strength shows to its best advantage— the strength, in fact, not only of his intellect but also of his will. He knew he was right, even if God did not. And he was not broken; four years later he is at it again, in a second series of *The Romance of Natural History,* incorporating more and more of the contemporary advances of science into his own scheme, never yielding an inch in his fidelity to the inspired word. Kingsley had also accused him of the apostasy of evolution: "I don't see how yours [i.e., Gosse's prochronism] differs from the transmutation of species theory, which your argument, if filled out fairly, would, I think, be."[43] Indeed there was a superficial similarity, but Gosse was careful to make the distinction for those who cared to look for it. Species may, without violating the sanctity of Scripture, *succeed* one another; they may not *evolve* from one another.

We know that the rate of mortality among *individuals* of a species, speaking generally, is equalled by the rate of birth, and we may suppose this balance of life to be paralleled when the unit is a species, and not an individual. If the Word of God contained anything either in statement or principle contrary to such a supposition, I would not entertain it for a moment, but I do not know that it does. I do not know that it is anywhere implied that God created no more after the six days' work was done. His Sabbath-rest having been broken by the incoming of sin, we know from John v. 17, that He continued to work without interruption; and we may fairly conclude that progressive creation was included as a part of that unceasing work.[44]

Gosse's devotion and ingenuity in the service of science and religion were unlimited; and in the end even the total indifference of both parties was not enough to stop his heroic rearguard action in defense of their divinely appointed unity.

IV

Edmund Gosse's charge against his father is that of inhumanity. "He regarded man rather as a blot upon the face of nature, than as its highest and most dignified development. . . . Among the five thousand illustrations which he painted, I do not think there is one to be found in which an attempt is made to depict the human form. Man was the animal he studied less than any other, understood most imperfectly, and, on the whole, was least interested in."[45] There is, in fact, at least one illustration containing human figures, but it only serves to reinforce the charge: the preface to *The Ocean* is accompanied by a woodcut of "The Whale Fishery," showing two men being tossed out of a boat into the jaws of a gigantic cetacean. As to the other assertions, Edmund may have been right—certainly his own experience led to no other conclusion. And yet it is perhaps too easy a judgment. One of the tragedies of an over-intellectual faith is that it may conceal, effectively and permanently, more natural feelings. Abraham, with his sons in his bosom, is a model of paternal affection, but it is a grim reflection that, had there been no ram in the thicket, nothing would have prevented him from murdering Isaac. Kierkegaard makes of Abraham a hero of faith, and the heroes of faith are generally those for whom, in the end, everything works out right, either in martyrdom or in earthly felicity. For Gosse, in a sense, nothing worked out right, yet his life, although it ended in dejection, did not end in defeat. As in Mr. Van Voorst's office, years before, his self-possession could be overcome only *in extremis.* He was, to use another favorite term of Kierkegaard's—a term of the highest approbation—an *individual;* and if his behavior as an individual was eccentric (as it undoubtedly was) that very fact made it, in spite of his frequently expressed wish to give all the credit to God, a tribute to the human strength of his own character.

Notes

1. Edmund Gosse, *Father and Son* (New York, 1907), p. 328.
2. Edmund Gosse, *The Life of Philip Henry Gosse, F.R.S., by his Son* (London, 1890), p. 72.
3. Edmund Gosse, *Father and Son*, p. 6.
4. Titian Peale, a painter of animals, is the only brother he mentions; Rubens and Rembrandt, who earlier had made important contributions to American natural history, were by this time considerably older than Gosse. The father of these three (and of eight other children also named after artists) was Charles Willson Peale, the famous portrait painter.
5. Philip Gosse, *Letters from Alabama (U.S.) Chiefly Relating to Natural History* (London, 1859). Letter XII deals with manners in the South, especially with slavery.
6. Edmund Gosse, *The Life of Philip Henry Gosse, F.R.S.*, p. 157.
7. Philip Gosse, *The Canadian Naturalist. A Series of Conversations on the Natural History of Lower Canada* (London, 1840), p. 2.
8. Edmund Gosse, *Father and Son*, p. 113.
9. P. H. Gosse (assisted by Richard Hill, Esq., of Spanish-Town), *The Birds of Jamaica* (London, 1847).
10. Philip Gosse, *The Romance of Natural History* (London, 1860), p. 270.
11. Edmund Gosse, *The Life of Philip Henry Gosse, F.R.S.*, p. 152.
12. *Ibid.*, p. 70.
13. *Ibid.*, p. 72.
14. Edmund Gosse, *Father and Son*, p. 97.
15. *Ibid.*, p. 71.
16. *Ibid.*, p. 99.
17. *Ibid.*, p. 84.
18. P. H. Gosse, *The Ocean* (Philadelphia, 1856), p. 101. (The title-page bears the inscription, "from the last London edition.")
19. Philip Henry Gosse, *A Naturalist's Rambles on the Devonshire Coast* (London, 1853), pp. 354-357. This is not, after all, quite the discovery Gosse thought it. *Johnstonella* was not a new genus, but a subgenus of *Tomopteris*, which had been named in 1825 by Eschscholtz. The species *catharina* is still recognized by some workers, although Gosse's drawing and description are too vague to provide clear identification, and the name *helgolandica* attached to a later and more accurate description by Greeff is more usual. What Gosse hoped would be called *Johnstonella catharina* is in fact called *Tomopteris helgolandica*— a disappointing sequel to so magnanimous a gesture. (I am indebted for the foregoing information to Mr. Frederick M. Bayer, Acting Curator of the Division of Marine Invertebrates, Smithsonian Institution.)
20. Edmund Gosse, *The Life of Philip Henry Gosse, F.R.S.*, p. 376.
21. Edmund Gosse, *Father and Son*, p. 346.
22. Edmund Gosse, *The Life of Philip Henry Gosse, F.R.S.*, p. 367.
23. Philip Henry Gosse, *Omphalos: An Attempt to Untie the Geological Knot* (London, 1857), p. 5.
24. A Greek word meaning "navel." The epigraph to *Omphalos* is from Aristotle's *Historia Animalium*, book VII.8, and in D'Arcy Wentworth Thompson's translation reads: "All animals, or all such as have a navel, grow by the navel." The idea is, clearly, to make an analogy between Adam as the microcosm, whose navel pointed to a birth which never took place, and the earth as the macrocosm, whose fossils similarly are signs of an unreal past; but this comparison is not taken up seriously in the book, there being only two casual references to the navel at pp. 289 and 334. One might therefore look for a deeper significance in the title, in keeping with various secondary uses of the Greek term, such as its application to the stone at Delphi which was supposed to represent the center of the earth. But Gosse's epigraphs, like his scriptural quotations, are often disappointingly irrelevant, and on the whole it seems unlikely that there is any more to the title than the obvious meaning referred to above.
25. Philip Gosse, *Omphalos*, pp. vii-viii.
26. Edmund Gosse, *Father and Son*, p. 116.
27. Philip Gosse, *Omphalos*, pp. 103-104.
28. *Ibid.*, p. 110.
29. *Ibid.*, p. 122.
30. *Ibid.*, p. 123.
31. John Donne, *Essays in Divinity*, ed. E. M. Simpson (Oxford, 1952), p. 18.
32. Philip Gosse, *Omphalos*, pp. 124-125.

33. *Ibid.*, p. 126.
34. *Ibid.*, p. vi.
35. *Ibid.*, p. 372.
36. *Loc. cit.*
37. *Ibid.*, p. 369.
38. Edmund Gosse, *The Life of Philip Henry Gosse, F.R.S.*, p. 280.
39. *Ibid.*, pp. 280-281.
40. *Ibid.*, p. 281.
41. John Henry Cardinal Newman, *Apologia pro Vita Sua* (London, 1864), p. 120.
42. Edmund Gosse, *Father and Son*, p. 118.
43. Edmund Gosse, *The Life of Philip Henry Gosse, F.R.S.*, p. 281.
44. Philip Henry Gosse, *The Romance of Natural History, Second Series* (London, 1861), p. 89.
45. Edmund Gosse, *The Life of Philip Henry Gosse, F.R.S.*, p. 349.

Swinburne, the *Spectator* in 1862, and Walter Bagehot

by W. D. PADEN

In his life of Swinburne, Edmund Gosse wrote[1] that "in his twenty-fifth year" (that is, before 5 April 1862), apparently through Monckton Milnes, the poet met Richard Holt Hutton, who had been for about half a year the part-proprietor and co-editor of the *Spectator,* and who "invited him to write, in prose and verse, for his paper." The most probable interpretation of this airy phrase is that Hutton invited Swinburne to submit some verses and critical prose, without any explicit promise of publication. He could scarcely say less, and he was not likely to say more; in any case, the consequences of the invitation will be canvassed in this note.[2]

During the year the *Spectator* printed seven poems signed by Swinburne,[3] which he may have submitted in one group, in April; we do not know. The other verse printed in the paper in 1862 may safely be dismissed, as not his. Professor Chew inferred[4] from the variations between the texts of three of the poems in 1862 and in *Poems and Ballads* (1866) that in the earlier year "Hutton was exercising, and Swinburne was submitting to, a political and moral censorship"; but one must object that the changes in "The Sundew" have no relevance, and the additional stanzas in "Faustine" and "A Song in Time of Order" may with at least equal probability be supposed insertions made after the poems' first publication. On 7 June appeared a respectful letter[5] over Swinburne's signature but explicitly representing the consensus of a number of men, in protest against the castigation that Meredith's *Modern Love* had received a fortnight earlier. To the letter Hutton appended a note in which he remarked that "we insert this gladly, from personal respect to our correspondent, whose opinion on any poetical question should be worth more than most men's," before passing on to a brief, staunch defense of the offending review. In sum, the beginning of the connection was auspicious.

Gosse wrote that "it is less easy to speak of the prose contributions, because they were anonymous. Were it not for passages in private letters,[6] it would be dangerous to assert, what, however, those familiar with Swinburne's early style could hardly question, that the series of five long articles on *Les Misérables* of Victor Hugo, and on *Les Fleurs du Mal* of Baudelaire, are his.[7] There are several others which I am privately certain are also Swinburne's, but I deprecate mere conjecture, and will not name them." He added in a footnote that according to his information no documents of the period which might throw light on the matter were extant in the office of the *Spectator*.

Being less decorous than Gosse, Professors Chew and Lafourcade made public their surmises concerning Swinburne's further contributions in prose. Chew wrote that "the evidence of Swinburne's early style is so convincing that I am willing to risk conjecture. I seem to see his hand in several, but of only one article am I positive . . . ." This single article was a review of Mrs. Browning's *Last Poems,* of which Chew wrote: "Such phrases as 'The impulse of her eager and rich imagination in an age of pale thoughts and weak instincts' or 'The vanishing of a genuine poetic force in this languid and pallid mental world' bear Swinburne's sign manual upon them. The review contains a brief suggestive passage on the contrast between the superficiality of feeling and the profundity of imagination. Mrs. Browning, the writer says —and again the turn of thought is Swinburne's—'yields herself almost with the lashed fury of a Pythoness' to feeling." Professor Chew believed that reviews of Sir Henry Taylor's *St. Clement's Eve* and Miss Rossetti's *Goblin Market and Other Poems* were much in Swinburne's manner: "that both poets were among those whom Swinburne delighted to honor makes his authorship the more likely." He felt less certain about reviews of *The Bothie of Toper-na-Fuosich* and of Clough's *Poems;* but he asked whether Swinburne's voice may not be heard in a notice of Richard Garnett's *Relics of Shelley,* a protest against the publication of scattered scraps of Shelley's verse. And he ended his discussion by saying that "whether these identifications be accepted universally or not, it is quite evident that in order to make his forthcoming *Bibliography of Swinburne* quite exhaustive Mr. T. J. Wise will do well to examine the columns of *The Spectator* of 1862 with the most painstaking attention." There is no sign in Wise's volumes that he felt any need to supplement the cautious revelation of his friend and literary collaborator, Edmund Gosse.

Nine years later Professor Chew repeated his views, in phrases sufficiently varied to require consideration: "I think it more likely that Hutton suppressed [the additional stanzas to 'A Song in Time of Order'] than that they were afterwards added by Swinburne, for they contain allusions to the red flag of revolution, to the iniquities of the papacy, to 'Buonaparte the bastard,' to the scandals of the French political prison at Cayenne, and to Austrian tyranny—dubious topics to offer to Hutton's circle of Tory readers. 'Faustine' was printed with the omission of stanza xxxiii, which contains an allusion to abnormal eroticism."[8] But Hutton had no circle of Tory readers; the reference indicates some fundamental miscomprehension of the man, his work, and his time. The *Spectator* in 1862 contained strongly phrased statements of idealistic dissatisfaction with almost all British institutions except the Throne, of which the occupant herself was not exempt from respectful censure.[9] True, these were accompanied by affirmations in behalf of Faith, then undergoing a siege by the forces of science and agnosticism—enemies which Hutton surveyed with courteous candor from a very broad theological position. After a young manhood of hearty Unitarian idealism, he had been attracted to the affirmations of the Rev. Frederick Denison Maurice, and he remained a follower of that harried inquirer throughout the remainder of his own long career.[10] But had the readers of the *Spectator* been Tories, Chew's argument would remain circular, for he assumes the point he desires to prove. And finally, one may scan stanza xxxiii of "Faustine" in vain for any "allusion to abnormal eroticism," unless it consists of the word *epicene.* An editor who had passed stanzas xxx and xxxi cannot be supposed to have balked at stanza xxxiii. To continue, Professor Chew was "willing to suggest that it is just possible that reviews of Henry Taylor's *St. Clement's Eve,* of Christina Rossetti's *Goblin Market,* and of Clough's work (two notices) are by him; that the earlier portions of a review of Richard Garnett's *Relics of Shelley* are so much in his manner as to make his authorship almost a certainty; and that beyond doubt he wrote the review of Mrs. Browning's *Last Poems.*"[11]

One year before this note appeared, M. Lafourcade had written that "la conjecture est ici dangereuse, car le style est la seule preuve que l'on puisse invoquer. Signalons toutefois qu'un compte rendu du 10 mai sur le *St-Clement's Eve* de Henry Taylor nous paraît être du à la plume de Swinburne. Certaines particularités de vocabulaire (par exemple: *sheet lightning* etc.) ne peuvent guère tromper."[12] He did not revert to the subject in his later volume upon Swinburne (1932).

In the past many attributions based on prose style have proved untrustworthy; and in this case the technique has special dangers, for the reviews in question were Swinburne's first attempts at professional prose, and might be expected to resemble his later work only to a degree. But more systematic objections must be raised. The attributions rehearsed above may be termed *uncontrolled;* they not only disregard the available non-stylistic evidence, but assume that such evidence leaves it equally probable that Swinburne did or did not write any particular review. They do not consider chronology. They do not consider the reviews as wholes, nor do they advert to the presence or absence of passages which it is unlikely or impossible that Swinburne wrote.

They do not take into account the fact that twinned adjectives, lyrical metaphors, theories about the creative imagination, and pleasure in the dramas of Henry Taylor and the lyrics of Christina Rossetti were not in 1862 confined to Swinburne. They include no attempt to discover what other men wrote for the *Spectator,* or were close associates of its editor at the time, nor any consideration of the probability that some of the reviews in question were written by such men.

These cavils need not be argued in relation to the two reviews of Clough, for those were written by Hutton himself. The present writer had obtained adequate proof for the attribution when he learned of two letters in the *Times Literary Supplement* of 1959 in which Mr. Robert H. Tener announced the discovery.[13] Mr. Tener's argument on the point may be repeated here concisely, in less tentative terms than those his modesty led him to employ. Hutton's well-known essay on Clough was published in the second volume of his *Essays Theological and Literary* in 1871, and suffered no significant subsequent change. In the single volume of his *Literary Essays* reprinted in 1896, the year before his death, the text on pages 291 to 296, inclusive, is almost identical with the *Spectator*'s review of *The Bothie* (25 January 1862); and the text on pages 286 to 290, inclusive, presents in more generous phrasing the central concepts of the *Spectator*'s review of the *Poems* (12 July 1862). Anyone aware of the close friendship between Clough and Hutton would, in fact, be surprised if the two reviews should be proved the work of anyone other than the editor.

Mr. Tener quoted an autobiographical narrative by Charles Henry Pearson, who affirmed that for nearly a year in 1861-1862 he "wrote an article a week, chiefly reviews of books" for the *Spectator.* He continued: "I also contributed some fugitive pieces of poetry. They were, however, overshadowed by two or three of Swinburne's, which first saw the light in the *Spectator.* I came more successfully into competition with Swinburne as a reviewer of Victor Hugo. I took the first part of *Les Misérables* [i.e., volumes 1 and 2], he the second [volumes 3 and 4].[14] My praise was much more jealously measured out; but Victor Hugo himself preferred my article, ascertained from Louis Blanc that I was the author, and wrote to thank me for it."[15] Of the half-dozen poems in the *Spectator* that may have been Pearson's, the less said the better. As for Louis Blanc, though he scrupulously refrained from political conspiracy of any kind during his exile in England, he was a friend and warm admirer of Hugo, and, being in close touch with men of letters, no doubt had made a point of discovering the authors of the reviews of *Les Misérables,* including that in the *Spectator,* and informing Hugo. Whether the Master implied in his letter to Pearson that Blanc had inquired at his request, we do not know; it is more probable that Pearson himself made the flattering assumption. It does not seem likely that Hugo would express any preference between two reviews of his work in one journal, and his estimate of Pearson's article, as far as we know it—"bien remarquable et bien élevé"[16]—suggests no particular enthusiasm; possibly Hugo expressed a preference for the *Spectator*'s first review over those in other journals, and Pearson, conscious of his rivalry with Swinburne, in some way misconceived the compliment. In July 1862 Pearson took over the editorship of the *National Review,* of which Hutton had until then been the editor; their relations remained cordial.

The *Spectator*'s fifth article on *Les Misérables,* a review of the authorized translation into English, Mr. Tener considered possibly Pearson's but "almost certainly *not* Swinburne's." Its latter paragraphs are pervaded by a liberal but gradualist political theory that cannot be supposed the poet's.[16a] Swinburne's study of Hugo, then, consisted of the three articles of 21 June, 26 July, and 16 August, only. In this connection the invaluable M. Blanc also seems to have been active. Much later the poet wrote to Gosse that the first letter he received from Hugo came "in the summer of '62. . . . It was written in acknowledgment—very far too kindly expressed—of some crude and overbold articles (not signed) on *Les Misérables* which he had actually been at the trouble to trace to my hand by inquiry after the author's name."[17] It seems clear, despite Swinburne's plural reference, that this first letter concerned only his first article, that of 21 June, and that later he sent copies of the second and the third to Guernsey, where they lay awaiting Hugo's leisure—or rather, since Hugo could not read English, the leisure of his entourage—for four months; for the Master's further letter of approval, which refers to two reviews, was dated 26 December 1862. "Ces remerciements n'étaient rien de plus que ceux que Victor Hugo adressait journellement à ses admirateurs, sans se préoccuper le moins du monde de leur existence particulière, de leur personnalité, ou de leur absence de personnalité."[18]

Mr. Tener also wrote that "a comparison of the August 2 review, *Relics of Shelley,* with Hutton's 'Shelley's Poetical Mysticism,' *National Review,* XVI (January 1863), 62-87 (revised for *Essays Theological and Literary*), will indicate a strong possibility of Hutton's authorship of that article, too. I am privately convinced that Hutton reviewed *Goblin Market,* also. I am much less certain, however, about the authorship of the review of Henry

Taylor, though I think that Swinburne probably wrote, as Chew says, the appraisal of Mrs. Browning's *Last Poems*. The passage in the latter article —'yields herself almost with the lashed fury of a Pythoness'—which Chew finds so telling is indeed persuasively Swinburne's." But in connection with the article on the *Relics of Shelley* one does not need to revert to the *National Review* of 1863, or even to the *Essays Theological and Literary*. To the text of his essay of 1863 Hutton later prefixed almost fourteen pages drawn from his review of Dowden's life of Shelley (*Spectator*, 11 and 18 December 1886), but otherwise it underwent no significant change during his lifetime. One may compare: ". . . the strange perfection of his pantheism . . . seems to us one of the central features of all his poetry. It shows senses of ethereal fire, an intellect of wonderful subtlety, a soul of pure magnanimity, but no shadow of divine responsibility, no consciousness of living under an eternal eye and will . . ." (*Spectator* [2 August 1862], p. 860) and "His Pantheism was sincere, and at times no doubt a kind of faith to him; but belief in a universal essence gave no solidity to the order of the world, no firm law to the flux and reflux of human desire, had no power to accept the command, 'Be still, and know that I am God'" (*Literary Essays,* 1896, pp. 186-87). There can be no doubt that the two passages, which form the climaxes of the two essays, were written by the same man, for they contain the same very special conception of Shelley's thought. And in any case, it cannot have been the Swinburne of 1862 who wrote, in the *Spectator*'s review of the *Relics of Shelley*, "There is much of Shelley's life, looked at as a whole, which relieves the naked naturalism of his theory of love."

Nor can Swinburne be supposed the author of the review of Mrs. Browning's *Last Poems*, for he would not have approved the regretfully patronizing view of Aeschylus and Sophocles implied in its climactic passage: ". . . her manipulation of Greek myths is often eminently striking. She opens, as it were, a chasm of infinite depth beneath them, showing the thin crust which after all separated them from the deeper thought of divine truth." Nor can it have been Swinburne, despite his admiration for cats, who selected for praise from *St. Clement's Eve* a girl's description of her dream of being a cat, and predicted "a well-deserved immortality" for the lines, spoken by a pampered feline,

> And I was fat and sleek, but in my heart
> There rose a long and melancholy mew,
> Which meant, "I must have mice."

Nor, in fine, can it have been Swinburne who described Miss Rossetti's lyric,

'A Birthday,' as a delicate trifle containing one line of true poetry, and urged her to attempt more worthy genres.

As divination from prose style has failed, another method may be brought forward. A man accepted as a reviewer by a Victorian editor usually was assigned a definite area to which he was expected to confine his efforts and from which he might expect other reviewers as a rule to be excluded. Swinburne was already widely read in French literature, and proud of his knowledge; in their first conversation he may be supposed to have mentioned it to Hutton. If he was regarded by the editor as anything like a regular contributor, and therefore given any kind of priority in a defined territory, he may be supposed to have written about French literature. Certainly, the four articles which we know to be his support such an assumption, for they deal with Hugo and Baudelaire.

During 1862 the *Spectator* printed twenty reviews,[19] which dealt in some way with France, her history and thought, her life, or her literature. Ten of these may be dismissed as irrelevant here (see Appendix A); the remaining ten, which deal with French literature, include the six reviews advanced by Gosse and four others on, respectively, Mme. de Gasparin's *Les Horizons Prochains* (22 February), M. Davésiès de Pontès' translation of *Childe Harold* into French (30 August), Armand Renaud's *La Griffe Rose* (13 September), and the journals of Eugénie de Guérin (18 October). The article on Mme. de Gasparin, a devout Calvinist, contains a thoughtful and bitter contrast between the relations of religious sects in England and in France; the article on Eugénie de Guérin presents her as "the highest ideal of the feminine nature which the Catholic faith, implicitly accepted, is capable of forming out of the purest and noblest material of the old French noblesse." In other words, the two articles deal with the religious life, rather than the literature which records it, and for that reason may also be dismissed from our consideration (see Appendix A, again).

The *Spectator*'s review of M. de Pontès' translation of *Childe Harold* contains nothing Swinburne might not have written. "Byron's rhetoric and artistic perfection," it runs, "are the result, not of elaborate polish, which might be imitated, but of genius, and a natural command of careless eloquence." If the phrase *artistic perfection* were qualified by the remark that in Byron it was subject to disruption by false notes and disintegration through loose structure—as the later epithet *careless* could be taken to imply —the estimate of Byron would be strictly consonant with Swinburne's in his preface to his *Selections from the Works of Lord Byron* (1866). The reviewer turns to a regretful censure of M. de Pontès by a definition of metrical effects in both English and French verse; the discussion shows a knowledge and a confidence that in 1862 few Englishmen shared with Swinburne. But the final step towards attributing the review to the poet, the step from possibility to proof, cannot be taken on the basis of the internal evidence.

Before discussing the review of Armand Renaud it is convenient to state our present knowledge of Swinburne's work for the *Spectator* and the circumstances in which his connection with the paper was severed, for the chronology and circumstances are pertinent to the later argument. He composed a careful article on Théophile de Viau, which Gosse thought doubtless written in 1862;[20] the most probable season seems to be the spring, when he also wrote his review of Baudelaire, another careful essay.[21] He may have written his skit on *M. Prudhomme at the International Exhibition* at any time after the great display opened on 1 May;[22] he submitted this to Hutton a noticeably long time before December.[23] During the spring and summer, in a footnote to his poem published on 24 May and in his reviews of 21 June, 26 July, and 16 August, Swinburne made a number of casual references to two fictitious Frenchmen, Ernest Clouët and Félicien Cossu,[24] and sometimes quoted from their works; and during the summer he wrote his highly indignant article on Clouët's scurrilous essays, which before 18 August not only had he lent or sent to Monckton Milnes to amuse him on his sickbed, but Milnes had returned.[25] This article he submitted to Hutton, one may guess in late August or September,[26] a season when the editor may have been out of London on his annual holiday. Swinburne's erotic preoccupation was increased by his long-anticipated acquaintance with the *Justine* of the Marquis de Sade, which he read for the first time a day or so before 18 August.[27] Doubtless in his first excited response to the Marquis, in September or October, he wrote his most startling and unprintable hoax, on the poems of Félicien Cossu and—elevated beyond prudence—submitted it also to Hutton.[28]

Swinburne went north to visit Milnes, and left Fryston on 13 December to stay with the Trevelyans at Wallington Hall, where he remained through 2 January 1863.[29] It was therefore at Wallington that he received Hutton's letter of 16 December,[30] and learned of the editor's amazement over the proofs of the article on Clouët, which he did not really think he could print. We know that in his reply Swinburne loftily affirmed that "sanity and decency are the two props of my critical faculty."[31] In one of his demure accounts of the incident Gosse wrote that the editor "expostulated severely with the poet, [though] not for attempting to hoax the *Spectator*, which Hutton does not seem to have suspected."[32] Hutton was described by a close friend as a man "perfectly fearless, entirely just up to his lights of honour, so unblemished that during a long life no one ever dared to whisper a word against him, essentially truthful and sympathetic, and entirely disdainful of all base things. But with all this, he was by no means a milksop, and could be very angry on occasion. He kept discipline among his contributors with an iron hand."[33] So far as one may judge, Hutton seems to have read Swinburne's climactic effort, on Félicien Cossu, after 16 December, possibly after he had consulted some friend with a more extensive vocabulary in demotic French; of his final letter to the poet we have as yet been vouchsafed only one clause, perhaps the mildest it contained: "Such verses would blow the magazine off the face of the earth."[34] Swinburne came south, and wrote to Monckton Milnes on 21 January, "Have you read *Salammbô? . . .* I want to review it somewhere; do you know of any place one could get for it? I don't want to send any more to the *Spectator*; I don't approve of their behaviour (e.g. never sending one one's own articles, and taking back books for review—notamment four volumes of *Les Misérables*[35]), and their principles offend my moral sense."[36]

For clarity, one should add Gosse's comment on the two articles on Clouët and Cossu: ". . . in these curious, and somewhat bewildering [productions] we see Swinburne satirizing the Podsnappery of the age which supposed all French literature to be of a subversive and horrible immorality, and at the same time indulging, by means of ironic censure, in a number of outrageously subversive sentiments of his own. . . ."[37]

It is noticeable that, for whatever reasons, Swinburne's reviews appeared in the *Spectator* much later in the year than one might expect. The tardiness may have been his own; but in later life he did not often retain his prose for repeated polishings, and one may suspect that Hutton was responsible for much of the delay. All the parts of *Les Misérables* had been published in Brussels by the end of June, yet Swinburne's reviews of the last four parts appeared on 21 June (dealing with Parts II and III), 26 July, and 16 August. (In contrast, Pearson's review of Part I, which was published towards the last of March, appeared on 12 April.) Swinburne wrote his article on Baudelaire in the spring; it appeared on 6 September. His skit on M. Prudhomme, which he may have written as early as the month of May, lay so long on the editor's desk that Hutton apologized when he returned it to the poet in mid-December in order to obtain his consent to a minor omission. In mid-December, in fact, Hutton held either two or three unpublished and unexamined manuscripts by the poet; his delays may explain why Swinburne did not, so far as we know, submit his essay on Théophile de Viau.[37a]

Actually, the four prose contributions to the paper that we know to be Swinburne's appeared regularly at a rate of one a month: to repeat, on 21 June, 26 July, 16 August, and 6 September. Four of his poems appeared between 29 April and 31 May; the rest appeared at something like a rate of one a month, on 28 June, 26 July, and 6 September. These facts suggest that during June Hutton came to consider Swinburne as a partial replacement on his staff for Pearson, who departed on the first of July to the *National Review*, though instead of an article a week, and occasional poems, Swinburne was to supply an article and a poem each month. That some gap existed between the two arrangements may be indicated by the *Spectator's* second review of *Les Miserables*, which seems a month late, and deals not with Part II merely, but with Parts II and III. If these very tentative suggestions have any validity, it is more likely that articles contributed by Swinburne but hitherto unidentified will be found in the issues of the latter half or latter third of 1862, rather than in those of the earlier months. One article that might be Swinburne's, the review of M. de Pontès that appeared on 30 August, has been discussed above; if it was the poet's, it increases the probability that others of nearby dates may be his—such as the review of *La Griffe Rose,* of 13 September.

But here again some preliminary matter should be inserted. The review of *La Griffe Rose* may have some connection with an earlier review of *Chateau Frissac; or, Home Scenes in France*, a novel written by an Englishwoman under the *nom de plume* of Chroniqueuse; the earlier review appeared on 8 March. It may be exhibited by a brief quotation:

Chroniqueuse has apparently pursued life as a fine art in France until she breathes its very atmosphere, while retaining, however, a clear perception of the great difference in tone and colour between it and the best English society of the same phase. She professes to point her moral against *mariages de convenance*. But, in fact, she writes as if it were an offence against the true *art* of life to contract marriages of mere external convenience, mainly because a "great passion," and a true affection in married life, are elements of so much higher value to society and to all the graces, than any external means, that it is a wanton sacrifice of the highest social influences, to put what are commonly called worldly considerations before those which lend to the world all its refinement and beauty. Such a course degrades life from a fine art into one of the vulgarer arts of physical utility. It is not then so much as *wrong,* but as an offence against the true art of social enjoyment, that this novelette appears to enter a protest against mercenary motives for the marriage contract. . . . The authoress says in her preface, that "in order to expose better the evils of the *mariage de convenance*," she has "per force touched upon subjects which, to the pure English mind, will, perhaps, seem somewhat *risqués.*" We must say that the scene in Madlle. X.'s rooms, to which principally allusion must be here made, so far from being essential to the drift of the story, is lugged in by head and shoulders, apparently without any object, except to lend this questionable interest to the tale, the general spirit of which is by no means objectionable.

The review of *La Griffe Rose* (13 September) must now be given in its entirety:

The state of French fiction has at length become such that it is scarcely possible to give in the English language and within the settled conventions of English writing, an accurate account of any of its more characteristic productions. The plot not only abounds in incidents, but essentially depends on relations between men and women which English books never mention, which Englishmen call *en masse* immoral, which none of us, without Continental assistance, would have the patience or the wish to pursue into their natural complexities. An English writer would consider he was advancing into debateable if not forbidden ground, if he treated of the events with which Sir Cresswell Cresswell is specially concerned.[38] Divorce and adultery are, perhaps, within the present limits of English art, if treated with rapidity and delicacy, and if admitted to be immoral. Not one in twenty even of our most popular novelists could handle such topics graphically and dramatically, and yet not overstep the prescribed boundaries. Almost every one would hazard some expression or venture on some dangerous scene, which would exclude his book from "family" perusal, and thereby deprive it of saleability, and him of his remuneration. We pay our writers to be moral; and they are moral. But the French have no such custom; on the contrary, a French novelist is rather expected to be immoral. Among the purchasers of such works, probably the majority would feel *hurt* if they contained no scenes which English morals would forbid, and which English women would shrink from. A mere infraction of the marriage vow is too trifling a peccadillo, if indeed it is even a peccadillo, to be the subject of an exciting narrative. Dumas *fils* has indeed contrived to render it proper for modern art. His *Roman d'une Femme* [1848] entirely turns on such on event; but he escaped the vice of commonplace by making the wife love her husband, and *not* love her lover all the while that she is guilty of adultery with her lover; and thus contrived to make the situation sufficiently *piquant.* The author of *Fanny*[39] went over to the side of the lover, showed what he considered to be a wife, his duties, and described his natural and suitable jealousy of the husband.[40] His book is intended for an inventory of the duties of a married woman towards the admirer whom she does love. In the novel before us, M. Renaud[41] has undertaken to delineate a phase yet more curious. *La Griffe Rose* is an account of the evil consequences which ensued from a married lady's not yielding sufficiently *soon* to the addresses of an admirer whom she does not love. She did yield at last, but it was too late. He committed suicide and she went into a convent.

If the plot is not English, its reflections and its fundamental view of life are more un-English still, if possible. Who can translate such sentiments as the following? "O grandes courtisanes de tous les temps! ils sont aveugles les philosophes qui vous insultent. Qu'ils amassent déclamations sur déclamations! ils n'empêcheront pas que le culte rendu par vous au luxe, à l'élégance, à tous les rayonnements de la forme, n'ait sa bonne influence, qu'en faisant de vos chambres une féerie, de vos toilettes un rêve vous ne developpiez le sens artistique; qu'il ne s'exhale de vos dentelles et de vos parfums un certain idéal élevant l'âme à sa manière, car tout chemin mène à Rome, et *toute beauté mène à Dieu*?" Perhaps no one attained to God that way before, with whomever *else* they may have connected themselves. A whole volume, too, of utterly un-English reflection may be summed up in the following description of a woman's marriage, "Son esclavage de fille est fini; elle est femme, c'est-à-dire, en bon français, *elle peut se laisser aimer.*"

Very many persons will say that such books ought not to be written; that, if written, they ought not to be read, that they express thoughts which it is unwise to think and delineate scenes which it is objectionable to imagine. As for the writing of such books, *we* have no call to say anything; the clever writers of them, if it is ever needful, will say all which can be said on that head much better than we can. It may not be much after all;—still it will be much more than anything we could say. But as to the reading of them, we think there are reasons why persons of sufficient age and sufficient moral stability should not eschew the practice.

In the first place, it is a rare advantage to find in a highly civilized age a really *frank* literature. Books seem at first to have been written for men only. They now scarcely seem to be written for men at all; they are written for every part of the species *except* men. The mode in which the change has happened is certainly very natural; the change itself was nearly inevitable, and perhaps, upon the whole, by no means undesirable. So long as the hard-headed men were, as in Greece and Rome, the principal part of the great literary public, all subjects could be discussed with the freedom of exclusively masculine conversation. No man at a club is afraid of hurting other men by explaining his meaning; he believes that they have encountered much before, and therefore will probably be able to hear what he wishes to say; he is sure that if his conversation will hurt them, their moral state must be so delicate that something else will impair it before the day is out, even if he hold his tongue. The old writers must have had much the same feeling. They wrote for men whose minds were seasoned, or were being seasoned; they wrote nearly as they talked, without much fear and very little reticence. We cannot write so now. We have taken young ladies into the club. Every remarkable work of fiction is certain at present to be read by many immature minds of the feebler sex before it has been many days published. On such minds an outspoken literature might easily produce very pernicious effects. A large experience proves that the moral constitution of the female mind loses its tone far more easily than the masculine; it is in the good sense and the bad a more delicate constitution. It is both more easily destroyed, and is finer and gentler while it lasts. There is a light bloom upon it which man's nature has not, but if that bloom is rubbed off,—and it is rubbed off very easily,—woman's nature becomes inferior to man's. We teach our boys to read novels, too, now-a-days, and we must be careful that there is not anything in them which we do not wish them to read. As civilization grows, literature is cramped; the fetters of a propriety are laid upon it, which our fathers had not to bear, and which hamper half its movements.

French literature is exempt from this defect, at any rate. Young ladies are not allowed to read novels in France, and do not read them. They marry earlier than here, and before marriage they are permitted very little liberty, —are prevented from knowing much, and are sedulously taught to seem to know less than they do. Writers in France, therefore, still retain much of the liberty of ancient writers. And though France is unquestionably injured by her habit in this matter, other nations may be benefited. Hardly any part of life can be well comprehended until it is imaginatively delineated. Even common persons who pass through it learn its facts, but do not learn its spirit; they are as superficial travellers, who see the mile-stones and the hedges, and the bats, but who know little of the broad country and rural population on either side of them. Those who have not themselves experienced any sort of life,—and there are many sorts of life which it is very undesirable to experience—are dependent on description of necessity. The *demi-monde* in London thrusts itself in our very faces; we see it in the parks and at the opera; but how are those who are too moral to associate with it to learn anything about it? Some people may come to think too much about it if it is always unknown, mysterious, and good-looking. They may, however, learn something from M. Dumas *fils* and his imaginative delineation of it. They may learn, at least, this—that it consists of human beings "like unto us," who are in part evil, but yet not all evil.

Secondly, and this is, perhaps, the more material consideration of the two, an observing student of French novels may easily learn from them the real consequence of several decent vices which exist among ourselves, but which are here too decent, are too much involved in the complexities of life, and too intermingled with other more innocent elements, to display their latent deformity. In France some of these vices are practiced on a great scale, as well as more openly, and their novelists who are cunning in the artistic development of immorality, display all their bad consequences without glozing over any and even with a sort of ardour. Take, for instance, the vice of immoral marriage, which is always one of the characteristic sins of a highly civilized society. It certainly is not unknown in England. Mr. Thackeray has proposed to call a "midnight meeting" in Belgravia of all the ladies in that quarter who have, as he phrases it, "*sold* themselves in marriage." He has pointed out what a respectable, genteel, fashionable, and multitudinous assembly it would be; in what "diamonds and Chantilly lace" its company would be clothed; what bishops went to their weddings; what a big room would be required to hold them.[42] Nor is this vice confined to the highest class; it goes down to the lowest steps of the social scale. Not long ago a woman in Somersetshire, who had married a most unpromising brute, and had been very ill-used by him, was asked, "However came you to marry this man?" "Oh, ma'am," she replied, with sobs, "he had a dresser *and that*." Yet although the existence of this vice is well known and obvious with us, its effects are disguised and latent. It is commonly the only considerable sin which a young lady has a chance of committing, and she very frequently commits it without reluctance. Still she hurts herself rather than us. She leads in appearance an unexceptionable life; society cannot discover the interior of women's minds, and cannot discriminate which of them love their husbands when they marry them and which do not. The acutest of us would probably be often deceived if we attempted to decide in particular cases where there was real affection and where there was none. And as we cannot be sure where the original fault has been committed, we cannot say what ill consequence it has or has not produced. Very often, as far as we can judge, it produces no bad public results whatever.

If a young lady sells herself to an old fool and does it decently, she is a discreditable young person leading a discreditable life, and that is the whole story. Such marriages being the exception, and not the rule, she goes to and fro among innocent women; she does some harm, of course; she lowers the tone of modesty as she passes; she thinks all men "much the same," and regards a decorous and regular vice as the ineradicable habit of the human race. Still the state of these ladies, though despicable, is not intolerable; they suffer little and they have nice dresses; it will not do to "point a moral." But French society is different. Marriages of affection are there the exception— the rare exception. Marriages of *convenance* and arrangement are the common rule. The writers of fiction trade upon this social fact; it is the central idea of their works, the staple out of which most of them are manufactured. We see in them clearly delineated—depicted, we may say, *ad nauseam*—the whole results of a social system in which a principal engine of moral good is turned into a principal engine of moral evil. "If water chokes a man," says the Greek proverb, "what shall he take after it?" If marriage itself leads men and women into sin; if, being contracted from base motives or bad feelings, it is itself a sin, what is to be done, how can the social evil be cured? The true salt has lost its savour, and where shall we seek a substitute? The inevitable consequences of such a sort of marriage are to be found in *Fanny* and *La Griffe Rose*. When a woman's relation to her husband becomes sinful, moralists or *quasi* moralists endeavour to inquire what should be her relation to her lover, and it cannot be said that they arrive at any very satisfactory result. (pp. 1029-30)

This review might be considered as Swinburne's first venture into a mischievous exposition of French literature for the English public according to English prejudices. During the summer, one might argue, he combined the *Spectator*'s earnest disapproval of *mariages de convenance* (as in the review of *Chateau Frissac*), the kind of startling quotations he was casually inserting in his reviews of Hugo (though here they are authentic), and his disdain for English social hypocrisies and especially for English literary hacks ("We pay our writers to be moral, and they are moral"), and by ironic treatment achieved a wicked pastiche of the *Spectator*'s pontifical moralizing. He could have sent the review to Hutton as early as June or July. The escalade, one may suppose, was tempting; he expanded his use of non-existent French authors, and during the same months wrote his mock-denunciation of Ernest Clouët ("the zealous chisel"?). He had already experimented with explicit irony in his skit on M. Prudhomme (which Hutton had not yet protested, and in December was to improbably accept): perhaps greater exploits in *blague* were possible? Excited by the ridiculous, the strangely welcome pages of *Justine* he embarked on an even more ferocious hoax, on Félicien Cossu ("the well-podded reveller"?), and in late August or September sent the two manuscripts to No. 1 Wellington Street, and awaited the result. He travelled to Fryston, to Wallington . . . before a perception of incongruity burst into Hutton's well-regulated consciousness. The sequence is persuasive. To be sure, as the review progresses the irony fades and almost disappears, so that the final paragraph is unambiguously stern. One may recall that about a year later, perhaps as early as the summer of 1863, Swinburne was to undergo a major psychological shock when his younger cousin Mary Gordon, with whom it seems clear he was deeply in love, told him of her engagement to a man twenty-one years her senior, a military hero who had lost his left arm at the siege of Multan in 1849.[43] It does not seem irrational to suggest that the marriage was arranged on Miss Gordon's behalf by her parents; and that some hint or prevision of the engagement may have perturbed Swinburne in the summer of 1862, and as he wrote gradually turned a jest into earnest.

The argument is plausible. The attribution seems consistent with the nature and chronology of the poet's known work for the *Spectator*, and may be considered as anchored by a reference to his innermost life. It is a fair example of an attribution to an author built up in disregard of the evidence not directly relevant to him. The technique is dangerous.

The notion that Victorian literature had become delimited in subject and treatment because of the admission of young ladies to the reading public was to be stated by Swinburne with much greater force in his *Notes on Poems and Reviews* (1866); but it was not peculiar to him. It had been discussed in the *Saturday Review* in 1859 by Leslie Stephen,[44] and was to be stated, in terms quite close to those employed in the review of *La Griffe Rose,* by Walter Bagehot in 1864, in his essay on Sterne and Thackeray.[45] The wide currency of the argument may plausibly be supposed to have been related to the innovations in Lord Campbell's Act for the suppression of pornographic books and prints (1857), which led to Sir Alexander Cockburn's famous and long-honored formulation of the test of obscenity, in the Hicklin case (1868)—"whether the tendency of the matter charged as obscenity is to deprave and corrupt those whose minds are open to such immoral influences and into whose hands a publication of this sort may fall"; Sir Alexander added in his charge to the jury that the pamphlet in question would "suggest to the minds of the young of either sex . . . thoughts of a most impure and libidinous character."[46] These facts do not disprove any ascription of the review to Swinburne, but they indicate that the argument has been inadequately controlled. Both Stephen and Bagehot were addicted to irony; and though Stephen does not seem to have had any connection with the *Spectator*, the reverse was true of Bagehot.

Bagehot and Hutton had become close friends as young men, when they were students at University College, in London. After Bagehot left the study of law for the family bank in Somerset he contributed a number of literary essays to the *National Review*, then edited by Hutton. In 1858 Bagehot had married the eldest daughter of James Wilson, the founder and owner of the *Economist*, and on his father-in-law's death succeeded him as its editor. Its office stood not far from that of the *Spectator*: "The connection between the papers naturally became close. 'I doubt if I ever received a letter from Mr. Bagehot in my life,' maintained Meredith Townsend [Hutton's co-editor]. 'If he had anything to say he ran into *The Spectator*, and if I had anything to say I ran into *The Economist*.' Once a week, when Hutton and Bagehot had put their respective papers to bed, they would adjourn to the Athenaeum for a game of chess."[47] Bagehot was an omnivorous reader of novels, as a means of relaxation, and pleaded with his five sisters-in-law to obtain them for him from the circulating libraries.[48] During their father's lifetime some of these ladies had supplied reviews of light literature to the *Economist*,[49] and may be supposed to have continued their work when Bagehot became the editor. As a rule the pages, and the "Literary Supplements," of the journal dealt with sterner stuff; during 1862 the *Economist* printed only seven reviews of novels, most of them brief and chatty. The review of Thackeray's *Adventures of Philip* (1 November), however, shows a penetration, an ethical severity, and and a distrust of the author, which strongly suggest the hand of Bagehot himself. The tardiness of the review, its length (which is unusual for a notice of a novel in the *Economist*), and the accidental presence within it of two lines of type from a different discussion,[50] all suggest that the review was written and inserted to fill a gap caused by the cancellation of other material. In fact, Bagehot had reviewed *The Adventures of Philip* almost three months before, in the *Spectator* of 9 August;[51] and there can be little doubt that in early September he was aware of Thackeray's attack upon the English marriage-market, which informs much of the first third of *Philip.*

It was the kind of thing that moved an old lady to say, "Mr. Thackeray is an uncomfortable writer"—and Bagehot, quoting her, to agree.[52] Bagehot had been raised, by a fortunate birth and a fortunate marriage, as well as his exceptional mind, to a significant position in the center of that upper middle class which then ruled England and her empire. He saw Thackeray as a man plagued by an oversensitivity to the actualities of English society which, because it was undisciplined by any intellectual analysis of the English social structure, led him to mourn sentimentally over the cruder manifestations of laudable social processes. The central principle of English society, Bagehot considered, was its system of *removable inequalities*: the opportunity it afforded English families to rise, by the accumulation of wealth and by prudent alliances, to acknowledged membership in the dominant class, which Bagehot often called, perhaps a trifle casually, *the world.* Snobbery, then, and the advantageous display of nubile daughters were necessary for the larger good, and acceptable, since they would be governed, Bagehot assumed, in general, by the decent compliance with good taste that a gentleman instinctively exercises. Of the final large qualification Thackeray protested himself unsure: an uncomfortable writer.

Yet the detachment and penetration that were Bagehot's most impressive intellectual virtues may well have led him, after a startled perusal of *La Griffe Rose*, to explore the converse argument and to publish the result in the convenient anonymity of the *Spectator.* The mischievous suggestion of a moral reason for reading immoral books was not beyond the man who in 1852 had perturbed the Unitarian readers of their special organ, the *Inquirer*, by seven letters from Paris in agile defense of the *coup d'état* of Napoleon III and the predominance of the Catholic Church in the French state. The speculative freedom of Bagehot's conversation, his uninhibited informal pursuit of truth, was gratefully remembered by all his intimates. The quotations from Thackeray's most scarifying recent paragraph, though somewhat muted, would come naturally from Bagehot's pen at this time. The review includes an anecdote of a Somersetshire woman which rather strongly indicates Bagehot as the author, for he grew up in Somerset and frequently returned to his father's house. The moral passion that darkens and strengthens the final paragraph of the review, if taken as his elaboration of Thackeray's position, seems strictly consonant with Bagehot's mind. In sum, the review contains nothing that negates an ascription to Bagehot, much that is consistent with such an ascription, and several things that indicate his hand.

One must conclude that these considerations balance, and indeed outweigh, the probability that the review of *La Griffe Rose* was written by Swinburne. The argument for Swinburne is tortuous and complicated by superadded hypotheses, each of which logically reduces the probability of the whole; the argument for Bagehot is in comparison simple and forthright, though also inconclusive.

And finally, if the review of *La Griffe Rose* cannot be attributed to Swinburne, the probability that the article on M. de Pontès was his becomes smaller, and we must turn towards the view that during April and May 1862 Hutton regarded the poet as a contributor of verse rather than of prose, and in June, when Pearson's departure for the *National Review* became imminent, came to think of Swinburne's rights and responsibilities as limited to one review and one poem a month—at the most, when Hutton was not too busy to examine his manuscripts, as Hutton soon became.

POSTSCRIPTUM. In the catalog of the Ashley Library (VII, 42), sub *Ernest Clouët,* Wise wrote, "Accompanying the galley proof are two letters from Hutton to Swinburne concerning *M. Prudhomme* and *Ernest Clouët.* The first is undated, the second is dated December 16th, 1862"; and he proceeded to quote from the second letter. Being in London, I thought it sensible to inspect the letters, which are now B. M. Ashley A. 1987, fo. 188-191. Unfortunately, the letter Wise averred to be undated bears the date 16 September 1862; and the letter he said bore the date 16 December 1862 bears no date whatsoever. (These letters will be published in Mr. Tener's forthcoming book on R. H. Hutton.)

The first letter makes several things clear: (a) To Hutton's knowledge, during August 1862 the *Spectator* had printed no article by Swinburne except his third essay on Hugo—which destroys the possibility that he wrote the reviews of M. de Pontès and Garnett. (b) Since Hutton alludes at length to the review of Baudelaire (6 September) but neither refers nor alludes to the review of Renaud (13 September), the possibility that the poet wrote the second is almost completely destroyed. (c) The skit which now centers in the figure of M. Prudhomme was written to deride one "Ignoramus" who described his visits to the International Exhibition in *All the Year Round* on 21 June, 23 August, 30 August, and later dates—and on 30 August (pp. 584-585) spoke severely about "the ecclesiastical decorative department" (which included stained glass by Morris, Marshall, Faulkner, & Co.), and compared it contemptuously to "those pictures by the Belgian Leys" (which had recently overwhelmed Gabriel Rossetti); neither, he pointed out, seemed to know of or joy in the March of Mind. Both sentences spoken by M. Prudhomme in the text we have ("wicked is the word for this" and "after all, we need not be very angry") are direct quotations from "Ignoramus." The skit, which until now has puzzled many readers by its apparent lack of point, was in fact similar in nature to Swinburne's polemics in *Under the Microscope:* it was a defense of his friends. (d) Since on 16 September Hutton was unwilling to publish the skit because he thought the public would not identify "Ignoramus" as its target, one must allow the possibility that the poet revised it to please the editor; it is possible that Messrs. Prudhomme and Coquardeau were made much more prominent, —conceivably, were introduced—in order to make clear the skit's tenor.

The second letter was published by Wise, except for four sentences in its third and final paragraph; it has long been known that Hutton later decided to use the skit set in the International Exhibition, and that the article on Clouët, read in galley-proof, had caused him to feel grave misgivings. Since this second letter bears no date, we cannot say when it was written; it could have been written at any time after 16 September. The sentences omitted by Wise make several things plain: (a) Swinburne had earlier applied for several volumes to review, including Leon Gozlan's *Balzac chez lui* (Paris, 1862), and his request had been either disregarded or forgotten by Townsend, the co-editor, during Hutton's absence (was his absence caused by a death in his family?—both letters are written on mourning stationery). (b) Hutton explained what (he believed) had happened, but offered for review neither the volumes Swinburne had requested nor any others. He said politely that he would like to see what Swinburne would say about Gozlan's book: which one must note does not amount to a commission to review it. In general Hutton made it quite clear that he was chary of offering further work until the poet had tidied up his aesthetics.

But where is Hutton's final letter, from which Wise quoted a sentence in 1920? That sentence is, apparently, the only available proof that Swinburne ever submitted to Hutton his article on Félicien Cossu. Once bitten, twice shy; perhaps one should decline to rely on Wise's assertion until one can inspect the manuscript of the purported letter? For that matter, where is Swinburne's letter to Hutton, in reply to one or the other of the letters paraphrased above, in which he maintained that "sanity and decency are the two props of my critical faculty"?—no other letters from Swinburne to

Hutton are known, or seem to have been known in the past: how can one explain Gosse's ability to quote from this one? Can it be possible that here again Gosse stepped beyond his documents? Suspicion is deplorably contagious; other matters rise in the mind. In his preface to the privately printed edition of Swinburne's article on Baudelaire (1913), Gosse wrote that the poet "told me he wrote the review 'in a Turkish bath,' and I thought he said 'in Paris.' But was he in Paris until March, 1863?" The suggestion does not occur in the relevant passage in Gosse's *Life;* indeed, its absence there should be considered an implicit rejection. Nevertheless the notion was reproduced by Lafourcade as a simple statement (*Jeunesse,* I, 200), with the explanation that Swinburne was in Paris in the spring of 1862 on his way to join his family in the Pyrenees. But—as Lafourcade of all scholars should have known—the usual mid-nineteenth-century route from England to the Pyrenees did not pass through Paris, but through Bordeaux. Therefore, one must reject as a ghost the idea that Swinburne wrote his review of Baudelaire in Paris in the spring of 1862; no doubt he wrote it in a Turkish bath, but we do not know where the bath was, or when he wrote the article. The manuscript of *Théophile* seems to have been sold by Wise even before Gosse helped him publish the text, in 1915; at least, Gosse does not imply that he ever saw it. The manuscript of *M. Prudhomme,* though catalogued in the Ashley Library, was not received by the British Museum. It is a relief to be able to add that the manuscripts of the essays on Clouët, Cossu, and Father Garasse are today among the Ashley MSS; and that the first two seem contemporary by their paper and their handwriting, while the third seems obviously later, as Gosse asserted.

What can be said on the basis of certain knowledge about the chronology of Swinburne's work for the *Spectator?* Beyond the dates of publication of the poems and the four authenticated essays, we know only that the essay on Clouët was written before 18 August, the skit set in the International Exhibition (in some form, possibly not the one that we have) between 30 August and 16 September. As for the essays on Théophile and Cossu, we lack proof that either was written in 1862, or was ever offered to Hutton. We do not know when or in what fashion the connection between the poet and the journal was broken, except that this occurred after 16 September; our documents allow the possibility that Hutton merely sent back the manuscripts of *Prudhomme* and *Clouët* with a polite intimation that he found them unsuitable, and that as early as 1 October 1862 Swinburne desisted from sending in his work or applying for more.

What does this revised summary of our certain knowledge suggest as to the nature of the connection between Swinburne and the *Spectator?*— That he was, at first, a contributor of verse only. Hutton published in five months as much verse by Swinburne as he published during the year from all other men; and no poet except Swinburne was allowed to sign his name to his work in the *Spectator's* grave pages. That in May, when Pearson became preoccupied with his new duties on the *National Review,* Swinburne was asked to take over the series of reviews devoted to *Les Misérables* during its serial publication, so that in June, July, and August he published three essays on the work. Beyond this, that he successfully pressed upon Hutton, as his contribution for September, the essay on Baudelaire, though the editor came to be plagued with second thoughts, and perturbed at the pollution of his pages by unjustifiable metaphysics. That Swinburne's fifth manuscript, on the International Exhibition, Hutton at first declined; and that his sixth article, on Clouët, moved the editor to return both the fifth and sixth and the galley-proofs of the latter, with finality. In this light the connection seems to have been as tenuous as the poet's irresponsible mockery would naturally lead one to suppose. It seems to have been overestimated by Gosse the prosperous journalist, and its rupture seems to have been overdramatized by Gosse the raconteur.

NOTES

1. Edmund Gosse, *Life of Swinburne,* in *The Complete Works of Swinburne,* Bonchurch Edition, XIX (1927), 83.
2. C. K. Hyder, "A. C. Swinburne," in *The Victorian Poets,* ed. F. E. Faverty (1956), p. 145, n. 10.
3. See Appendix B.
4. S. C. Chew, "Swinburne's Contributions to *The Spectator* in 1862," *Modern Language Notes,* XXXV (1920), 118-119.
5. *The Swinburne Letters,* ed. Cecil Y. Lang (1959—in progress), I, 51-53.
6. Gosse must have referred to, among others, the letter from Swinburne to Monckton Milnes (Gosse, *Life,* 84-85) and that from Rossetti to Skelton (Georges Lafourcade, *La Jeunesse de Swinburne, 1837-1867,* Paris, 2 vols., 1928; I, 185), which make certain that Swinburne published an indefinite number of articles on Hugo, and the letter from Baudelaire to Swinburne which refers to the article on *Les Fleurs du Mal* as his (Lafourcade, *Jeunesse,* I, 210).
7. See Appendix B.
8. S. C. Chew, *Swinburne* (1929), p. 45n.
9. E.g., in the paragraph on the marriage of the Princess Alice in "The Week at Home" for 5 July.
10. In the *Spectator* of 1862 Bishop Colenso's famous attack on the arithmetic of the Pentateuch was reviewed with respect and firm disagreement on 8 November; it was discussed in "Veracity.—A Dialogue between a Jew and a Christian," signed by F. D. Maurice, on 29 November; the rigid reprobation of Colenso in the December issue of the *Church and State Review* was coolly and contemptuously denounced in an article entitled "Plumstead Episcopi on Heresy and Schism" on 20 December; and in the issue of 27 December Matthew Arnold's essay on Colenso in *Macmillan's* was, to speak plainly, eviscerated. Hutton's loyal admiration was also shown by the reviews he published of Maurice's *History of Modern Philosophy* (3-10 May); *The Sacrifices which we owe to God and His Church* (29 November); and *Dialogues between a Clergyman and a Layman on Family Worship* (20 December); and the attack upon Maurice's enemies in "Theology for Licensed Victuallers" (15 November).

11. Chew, *Swinburne*, p. 48n.
12. Lafourcade, *Jeunesse*, I, 198.
13. *TLS*, 24 April, p. 241, and 25 December, p. 755.
14. Bibliothèque Nationale, *Victor Hugo: Exposition* . . . (Paris, 1952). *Les Misérables* was published in five parts and ten volumes between the end of March and the end of June, 1862, at Brussels.
15. *Charles Henry Pearson, Memorials,* ed. William Stebbing (1900), p. 94.
16. The same, p. 143.
16a. The point can be proved by Swinburne's own statement: on 18 August he wrote to Milnes, "Have you seen *the rest* of my review of Hugo?"—*The Swinburne Letters*, I, 58; italics supplied.
17. A. C. Swinburne, *A Study of Victor Hugo*, ed. Edmund Gosse (1914), p. vii.
18. G. Jean-Aubry, "Victor Hugo et Swinburne," *La Revue Politique et Littéraire: Revue Bleue*, LXX (1936), 151. In this connection the only problem now unsolved is how to reconcile Gosse's statements in *A Study* and the *Life*.
19. For the sake of brevity, the argument here excludes the numerous articles on France that appeared in the *Spectator* as "Topics of the Day." Only one deals with literature: the description of Michelet's *La Sorcière* as an index of rising anticlericalism (13 December). Conversely, among the work Swinburne is known to have written or submitted to the paper, only the skit on *M. Prudhomme at the International Exhibition* could have been designed as a "Topic"; it resembles such jocular items as "The British Umbrella" (13 September) and "The Battle of the Guelphs and Ghibellines in Hyde Park" (11 October). No doubt Hutton accepted it as a bit of humor, a field in which he was not endowed with either talent or discrimination. The further argument in the text confines itself to the *Spectator*'s reviews.
20. T. J. Wise, *The Ashley Library*, VII (1925; henceforward, Wise B), p. 39. On the bases of paper and handwriting Gosse decided (Wise B, p. 40) that Swinburne wrote his essay on Father Garasse, the persecutor of Théophile, in 1865 or 1866—see Hyder, *Literary Career*, p. 271, n. 36.
21. Lafourcade, *Jeunesse*, I, 200.
22. T. J. Wise, *A Bibliography of Swinburne*=Bonchurch Edition, XX (1927; henceforward Wise C), p. 317.
23. Wise B, p. 42.
24. C. K. Hyder, *Swinburne's Literary Career and Fame* (1933), pp. 10-11; Tener, p. 755.
25. *Swinburne Letters*, I, 58.
26. Wise B, p. 42.
27. *Swinburne Letters*, I, 53.
28. See note 31. Possibly Swinburne sent in his last MS in October, in sheer pique, when the paper failed to print either of the efforts he had already submitted.
29. *Swinburne Letters*, I, 62, 63n, 68.
30. Wise B, p. 42.
31. Gosse, *Life*, p. 91.
32. Wise C, pp. 373-374.
33. William B. Thomas, *The Story of the Spectator* (1928), p. 67; compressed. Thomas' account of Swinburne's connection with the paper is wildly wrong.
34. T. J. Wise, *A Bibliography of Swinburne* (2 vols., priv. pr., 1919-1920), II, 400. Though Gosse always implies that the article on Cossu was sent to Hutton, the only available evidence seems to be this reference to *verses*: the other articles submitted by the poet contain no verses. The articles on Clouët and Cossu are now available in R. W. Hively, *A. C. Swinburne as a Literary Critic* (diss. Florida, 1958), of which a copy may be obtained from University Microfilms.
35. That is, the original volumes 3-10, containing the four *Parts* II-V; a corroboration of Pearson's claim that he, not Swinburne, reviewed Part I.
36. *Swinburne Letters*, I, 72.
37. Wise C, 377. On this point, one should now consult Walter E. Houghton, *The Victorian Frame of Mind* (1957), pp. 353-371, and Norman St. John-Stevas, *Obscenity and the Law* (1956), ch. III.
37a. There seems to be no evidence behind Lafourcade's assertion (*Jeunesse*, I, 199-200) that *Théophile* was submitted and rejected.
38. Sir Cresswell Cresswell was the first judge in ordinary and organizer of the new Court of Probate and Divorce in 1858-1863 (*DNB*).
39. *Fanny, une Étude par Ernest Feydeau* (1858), a sensational first novel.
40. Someone, probably a compositor, has created confusion here. The clauses should read

something like the following: "considered the situation from the viewpoint of the lover, indicated to the wife her duties to the lover, and described his jealousy in terms of that usually attributed to a husband." The description was sufficiently correct: but in this regard the book was a *tour de force*. Feydeau was no monster, but a petty acquaintance of Flaubert; no rattlesnake, but a wasp. His next novel, *Daniel* (2 vols., Paris, 1859), was chaste, pious, and sentimental. See Bernard Weinberg, *French Realism: The Critical Reaction* (1937), pp. 177-180.

41. "Renaud, Armand, administrateur et littérateur français, né a Versailles le 29 juil. 1836. Fils d'un medecin, il se consacra à la poésie, à l'imitation d'Émile Deschamps auquel il était attaché. Entré a l'Hôtel de Ville de Paris en 1860, il y fit un carrière administrative et fut chargé, en 1880, de la direction du service des beaux-arts à la prefecture de la Seine; il est devenu en 1889 inspecteur en chef de ce service. M. Renaud a publié: *les Poèmes de l'amour* (1860); *la Griffe Rose* (1864); [*les Caprices de boudoir* (1864); *les Pensées tristes* (1865);] *les Nuits persanes* (1870); *Recueil intime* (1881); *Drames du peuple* (1885)."—*La Grande Encyclopédie*. *La Griffe Rose* is (understandably) not mentioned in the histories of the French novel. The quotations are from pp. 203-204 and p. 183, respectively; the *Spectator*'s reviewer seems not to have read Renaud's last eighty pages, for his summary of the plot is incorrect. The novel consists of an arrangement of lyrical descriptions, in praise of an "idealized sensuality," which do not conceal a cold scepticism.

42. *The Adventures of Philip*, ch. 9, paragraph 9: "Well, I am not mortally angry with poor Traviata tramping the pavement, with the gas-lamp flaring on her poor painted smile, else my indignant virtue and squeamish modesty would never walk Picadilly or get the air. But Lais, quite moral and very neatly, primly, and straitly laced;—Phryne, not the least dishevelled, but with a fixature for her hair, and the best stays, fastened by mamma;—your High Church or Evangelical Aspasia, the model of all proprieties, and owner of all virgin-purity blooms, ready to sell her cheek to the oldest old fogey who has money and a title;—*these* are the Unfortunates, my dear brother and sister sinners, whom I should like to see repentant and specially trounced first. Why, some of them are put into reformatories in Grosvenor Square. They wear a prison dress of diamonds and Chantilly lace. Their parents cry, and thank Heaven as they sell them; and all sorts of revered bishops, clergy, relations, dowagers sign the book and ratify the ceremony. Come! let us call a midnight meeting of those who have been sold in marriage, I say, and what a respectable, what a genteel, what a fashionable, what a brilliant, what an imposing, what a multitudinous assembly we will have; and where's the room in all Babylon big enough to hold them?" It is noticeable that the sharpest thrusts of this paragraph do not appear in the *Spectator*.

43. Cecil Y. Lang, "Swinburne's Lost Love," *PMLA*, LXXIV (1959), pp. 123-130.

44. Both are quoted by St. John-Stevas—Swinburne, pp. 62-63; Stephen, p. 58.

45. *Literary Studies*, ed. R. H. Hutton (2 vols., 3rd ed., 1884), II, 120: "The audience has changed; and decency is of course in part dependent on who is within hearing. A divorce case may be talked over across a club-table with a plainness of speech and development of expression which would be indecent in a mixed party, and scandalous before young ladies. Now a large part of old novels may very fairly be called club-books; they speak out plainly and simply the notorious facts of the world, as men speak of them to men. Much excellent and proper masculine conversation is wholly unfit for repetition to young girls; and just in the same way, books written—as was almost all old literature,—for men only, or nearly only, seem coarse enough when contrasted with novels written by young ladies upon the subjects and tone of the drawing room. The change is inevitable; as soon as works of fiction are addressed to boys and girls, they must be fit for boys and girls; they must deal with a life which is real so far as it goes, but which is yet most limited; which deals with the most passionate part of life, and yet omits the errors of the passions; which aims at describing men in their relations to women, and yet omits an all but universal influence which more or less distorts and modifies all these relations." Cf. the fourth paragraph of the review. The passage occurs in Bagehot's discussion of *Tristram Shandy*, to whose sentiment he responded strongly, from whose indecency he shrank repelled; his nomination as *Victorianum maxime* could be justified by his complete inability, though himself an ironist, to discover Sterne's purpose in juxtaposing the two.

46. See St. John-Stevas, pp. 66-70, 126-128. The young ladies were immortalized by Dickens in the figure of Miss Podsnap.

47. Norman St. John-Stevas, *Walter Bagehot* (1959), p. 14.

48. Alastair Buchan, *The Spare Chancellor* (1960), p. 241.

49. The same, p. 104.

50. The review fills about two-thirds of page 1212, and four lines of type on page 1213; the first two lines on the second page read: "Now these views, though in the same direction as those of land-/owners of the first class, yet halt far beyond them. Lord Lichfield"—obviously,

because the new material was two lines of type short, two lines from the previous setting were accidentally retained.

51. Walter Bagehot, *The Works and Life* (ed. Mrs. Russell Barrington; 10 vols., 1915), IX, 282-286. This is the only contribution to the *Spectator* printed in the *Works;* its origin is correctly noted in the table of contents.

52. The paragraph is based on Bagehot's discussion of Thackeray in his essay on "Sterne and Thackeray" (1864).

Appendix A

REVIEWS IN THE *SPECTATOR* OF 1862 OF BOOKS CONNECTED WITH FRANCE, NOT CONSIDERED IN THIS NOTE

22 February   *Les Horizons Prochains, les Horizons Célestes, et Vesper.* Par Madame de Gasparin (London: D. Nutt). See page 97.

1 March   *Democracy in America.* By M. de Tocqueville. Translated by H. Reeve, Esq. A new edition, with an Introductory Notice by the Translator (London: Longmans).

8 March   *Chateau Frissac; or, Home Scenes in France.* By Chroniqueuse, Authoress of *Photographs of Paris Life* (London: Tinsley Brothers). See page 100.

8 March   *Mémoires de la Cour d'Espagne sous le Règne de Charles II., 1678-1682.* Par le Marquis de Villars (London: Trübner and Co.).

15 March   (Second notice of Villars.)

16 August   *Madame Duplessis Mornay, née Charlotte Arbalest.* Par Adolphe Scheffer (Paris: Cherbulier).

23 August   *Autobiography of a French Detective from 1818 to 1858.* By M. Canler (London: Ward and Lock).

30 August   *Histoire du Consulat et de l'Empire, faisant suite à l'Histoire de la Révolution Française.* Par M.A.Thiers. Tome XX (Paris: Paulin).

30 August   *An Essay on the Age and Antiquity of the Book of Nebathaean Agriculture. To which is added, An Inaugural Lecture on the Position of the Shemitic Nations in the History of Civilization.* By M. Ernest Rénan, Membre de l'Institut, &c. (London: Trübner and Co.).

6 September   *Souvenirs d'un Exilé en Sibérie* (Le Prince Eugène Obolenski). Traduit du Russe par le Prince Augustus Galitzin (Leipzig: Frank'sche Verlags-Handlung).

18 October   *Eugénie de Guérin. Journal et Lettres publiés avec l'assentiment de sa Famille.* Par G. S. Trebutien (Paris: Didier). See page 97.

6 December   *Souvenirs de Soixante Années.* Par E. Delécluze (Paris: Levy); and *Louis David; son Ecole et son Temps.* Par E. Delécluze (Paris: Didier, 1855).

Appendix B

TABLE OF REVIEWS ADVANCED AS BY SWINBURNE, AND HIS POEMS, IN THE *SPECTATOR*

25 January   *The Bothie of Toper-na-Fuosich:* just possibly by ACS (Chew); proved to be by Hutton (Tener).

29 March   Mrs. Browning's *Last Poems*: by ASC (Chew) By ACS? (Tener); shown not to be by ACS (Paden).

12 April   *Les Misérables, Pt. I:* by ACS (Gosse); proved to be by Pearson (Tener).

          Goblin Market: just possibly by ACS (Chew); by Hutton? (Tener); shown not to be by ACS (Paden).

29 April   *A Song in Time of Order*

10 May   *St. Clement's Eve:* just possibly by ACS (Chew); by ACS (Lafourcade); shown not to be by ACS (Paden).

17 May   *Before Parting*

24 May   *After Death (Breton)*

31 May   *Faustine*

7 June   (Letter on *Modern Love*)

21 June   *Les Misérables, Pts. II and III:* claimed correctly for ACS (Gosse)

28 June   *A Song in Time of Revolution*

12 July   Clough's *Poems*: just possibly by ACS (Chew); by Hutton? (Tener); proved to be by Hutton (Paden).

26 July   *Les Misérables, Pt. IV:* claimed correctly for ACS (Gosse).

                               The Sundew

2 August   Garnett's *Relics of Shelley*: almost certainly in part by ACS (Chew); by Hutton? (Tener); proved to be by Hutton (Paden).

16 August   *Les Misérables, Pt. V:* claimed correctly for ACS (Gosse).

30 August   M. de Pontès' *Childe Harold:* possibly by ACS (Paden).

6 September   *Les Fleurs du Mal:* claimed correctly for ACS (Gosse).

                               August

13 September   *La Griffe Rose:* by ACS? by Bagehot?—more probably by the latter (Paden).

25 October   "Victor Hugo's Philosophy," rev. of the authorized translation into English: by ACS (Gosse); almost certainly not by ACS—by Pearson? (Tener); not by ACS (Paden).

Index

117

Clough, Arthur Hugh, *The Bothie of Toperna-Fuosich*, 92, 93, 94; *Poems*, 92, 93, 94
Cockburn, Sir Alexander, 106
Cohen, Morris, 39
Coleridge, Samuel Taylor: politics disliked by Hazlitt, 1; Hazlitt's censure of, 5, 8, 18; "Christabel" admired by Hazlitt, 8; separation of "the Good" and "the Beautiful," 9; political views attacked by Hazlitt, 14; reads Wordsworth's poems to Hazlitt, 15 —"Christabel," 8; "The Rime of the Ancient Mariner," 6, 8
Compagnacci, 62
Congress of Vienna, 14
"consequitive reasoning," Keats's phrase, 6
Coriolanus, 6, 7
Cossu, Félicien, 98, 105, 109, 110
Cottington, Francis, Lord, 28
Coventry, 67
Cowley, Abraham, 4
Cross, John W., *George Eliot's Life*, 66
Crosse, Andrew, 69

Dallas, Ala., 70
Darby, John Nelson, 69, 75
Darwin, Charles Robert, 72, 79
DeVane, William Clyde, 24
"diachronic," 84, 85
Dissent Movement, 56
Donne, John, 83
Dowden, Edward, *Life of Shelley*, 96
Dumas, Alexandre *(fils)*, *Roman d'une Femme*, 101, 103

Economist, the, 106
Eliot, George: two kinds of intruder defined, 55; theological alienation, 56-58; role of compassion in community, 58-61; non-English intruders, 61-63; women intruders, 63-66; solitary childhood, 66-67; rejection of Church, 67; status in 1850's, 67
—*Adam Bede*, 55-68 passim; *Daniel Deronda*, 55-68 passim; *Felix Holt*, 55-68 passim; *Middlemarch*, 55-68 passim; *The Mill on the Floss*, 55-68 passim; *Romola*, 55-68 passim; *Scenes of Clerical Life*, 55-68 passim; *Silas Marner*, 55-68 passim
Elysium, 13
emotion, 3, 4, 5, 7
Encyclopaedia Britannica, 9
Erebus, 12
Essex, Robert Devereux, Earl of, 32
Evangelical Movement, the, 56, 66
Evans, Mary Ann. See Eliot, George
Evans, Robert, George Eliot's father, 67
Examiner, the, 2, 11, 13
Exhibition, International, 108, 109, 110, 111
experience, common, 3

Feydeau, Ernest, *Fanny*, 101
Fiennes, Nathaniel, 30, 31
Firth, C. H., 24, 25, 26

Flaubert, Gustave, *Salammbô*, 99
Florence, Italy, 62, 63, 65
Forster, John, *Life of Strafford*, 24, 25, 32, 67
free life, concept of, 40, 41, 43, 44
French literature, differences from English literature, 101-4
French Revolution, origin of poetry of paradox, 1; emphasis on abstractions, 4; responsible for Liberalism, 39
Froude, J. A., 67
Fryston, England, 98, 105
Furnivall, F. J., 24

Garasse, Father, 110
Gardiner, R. S., 27
Garnett, Richard, 92, 108; *Relics of Shelley*, 92, 93, 95, 96, 97
Gasparin, Mme. de, *Les Horizons Prochains*, 97
Genesis, 80, 82, 84, 85
Gifford, William, 14
Gillispie, Charles Coulston, 81
God, Philip Henry Gosse's concept of, 76, 77, 79, 81-88
Godwin, William, 5, 18
Gordium, 80
Gordon, Mary, 105
Gosse, Edmund: *Father and Son*, 69, 70, 76, 78, 79, 81, 87, 88; *Life of Swinburne*, 91, 92, 97, 98, 110, 111
Gosse, Elizabeth, 74, 78
Gosse, Philip: childhood, 70; interest in nature, 70-71; elected to Royal Society, 72; publications until 75 years old, 72; careful observations as a scientist, 72-73; speculations and reading tastes, 73; quotes the Bible, 73-74; illness of his sister Elizabeth, 74; rejects Goldsmith's remark on the lobster, 76, 77; names the *Johnstonella Catharina*, 77, 89; his prayers, 78; marries Emily Bowes, 75, 76, 78, 79; interest in evangelical preaching, 74, 75; relationship to his son Edmund, 71, 76, 78, 79, 88; concept of God, 76, 77, 79, 81-88
—*Actinologia Britannica*, 72; *The Canadian Naturalist*, 71; *Illustrations of the Birds of Jamaica*, 72, 73; *A Naturalist's Rambles on the Devonshire Coast*, 77, 89; *The Ocean*, 76, 88; *Omphalos*, 80-87; *The Prehensile Armature of the Papillonidae*, 72; *The Romance of Natural History*, 73, 74, 87
Gothic novel, 73
Gozlan, Leon, *Balzac chez lui*, 109
Green, Thomas Hill: influence upon later political thinkers, 39, 50-52; religious orientation, 42, 43, 50, 51, 52; self-consciousness, 42, 43; concept of the state, 42, 43, 44, 46, 48, 49, 50, 52; influenced by Kant and Hegel, 46, 47, 48, 49, 50; influenced by Ruskin and Carlyle, 45, 46; on Caesar, 50; on Napoleon, 49, 50; use of "moral,"